# Workshop on Language Analysis in Social Media 2013



## Atlanta, Georgia, USA
## 13 June 2013

ISBN: 978-1-62748-999-7

**Printed from e-media with permission by:**

Curran Associates, Inc.
57 Morehouse Lane
Red Hook, NY 12571



Printed by Curran Associates, Inc. (2013)

For permission requests, please contact the Association for Computational Linguistics at the address below.

Association for Computational Linguistics
209 N. Eighth Street
Stroudsburg, Pennsylvania 18360

Phone: 1-570-476-8006
Fax: 1-570-476-0860

acl@aclweb.org

**Additional copies of this publication are available from:**

Curran Associates, Inc.
57 Morehouse Lane
Red Hook, NY 12571 USA
Phone: 845-758-0400
Fax: 845-758-2634
Email: curran@proceedings.com
Web: www.proceedings.com

NAACL 2013

# Proceedings of the
# Workshop on Language Analysis in Social Media

13 June 2013
Atlanta, Georgia

# Introduction

These proceeding contain the papers presented at the workshop on Language Analysis in Social Media (LASM 2013). The workshop was held in Atlanta, Georgia, USA and hosted in conjunction with the 2013 Conference of the North American Chapter of the Association for Computational Linguistics-Human Language Technologies (NAACL-HLT 2013).

Over the last few years, there has been a growing public and enterprise interest in social media and their role in modern society. At the heart of this interest is the ability for users to create and share content via a variety of platforms such as blogs, micro-blogs, collaborative wikis, multimedia sharing sites, and social networking sites. The unprecedented volume and variety of user-generated content as well as the user interaction network constitute new opportunities for understanding social behavior and building socially-aware systems.

The Workshop Committee received several submissions for LASM 2013 from around the world. Each submission was reviewed by up to four reviewers. For the final workshop program, and for inclusion in these proceedings, nine regular papers, of 11 pages each, were selected.

This workshop was intended to serve as a forum for sharing research efforts and results in the analysis of language with implications for fields such as computational linguistics, sociolinguistics and psycholinguistics. We invited original and unpublished research papers on all topics related the analysis of language in social media, including the following topics:

- What are people talking about on social media?
- How are they expressing themselves?
- Why do they scribe?
- Natural language processing techniques for social media analysis
- Language and network structure: How do language and social network properties interact?
- Semantic Web / Ontologies / Domain models to aid in social data understanding
- Language across verticals
- Characterizing Participants via Linguistic Analysis
- Language, Social Media and Human Behavior

This workshop would not have been possible without the hard work of many people. We would like to thank all Program Committee members and external reviewers for their effort in providing high-quality reviews in a timely manner. We thank all the authors who submitted their papers, as well as the authors whose papers were selected, for their help with preparing the final copy. Many thanks to our industrial partners.

We are in debt to NAACL-HLT 2013 Workshop Chairs Luke Zettlemoyer and Sujith Ravi. We would also like to thank our industry partners Microsoft Research, IBM Almaden and NLP Technologies.

May 2013
Atefeh Farzindar
Michael Gamon
Meena Nagarajan
Diana Inkpen
Cristian Danescu-Niculescu-Mizil

**Organizers:**

Cristian Danescu-Niculescu-Mizil, Stanford University and Max Planck Institute SWS
Atefeh Farzindar, NLP Technologies
Michael Gamon, Microsoft Research
Diana Inkpen, University of Ottawa
Meenakshi Nagarajan, IBM Almaden

**Program Committee:**

Cindy Chung (University of Texas)
Munmun De Choudhury (Microsoft Research)
Jennifer Foster (Dublin City University)
Daniel Gruhl (IBM Research)
Kevin Haas (Microsoft)
Guy Lapalme (Université de Montréal)
Eduarda Mendes Rodrigues (University of Porto)
Alena Neviarouskaya (University of Tokyo)
Nicolas Nicolov (Microsoft)
Alexander Osherenko (University of Augsburg)
Patrick Pantel (Microsoft Research)
Alan Ritter (University of Washington)
Mathieu Roche (Université de Montpellier)
Victoria Rubin (University of Western Ontario)
Hassan Sayyadi (University of Maryland)
Amit Sheth (Wright State)
Scott Spangler (IBM Research)
Mike Thelwall (University of Wolverhampton)
Alessandro Valitutti (University of Helsinki)
Julien Velcin (Université de Lyon)
Emre Kiciman (Microsoft Research)
Valerie Shalin (Wright State)
Ian Soboroff (NIST)

**Invited Speaker:**

Mor Naaman, Rutgers University

# Table of Contents

**This page intentionally left blank.**

# Conference Program

**Thursday, June 13, 2013**

| | |
|---|---|
| 9:00–9:15 | Introductions |
| 9:15–10:30 | Invited Key Note, Prof. Mor Naaman |
| 10:30–11:00 | Coffee Break |
| 11:00–11:30 | *Does Size Matter? Text and Grammar Revision for Parsing Social Media Data*<br>Mohammad Khan, Markus Dickinson and Sandra Kuebler |
| 11:30–12:00 | *Phonological Factors in Social Media Writing*<br>Jacob Eisenstein |
| 12:00–12:30 | *A Preliminary Study of Tweet Summarization using Information Extraction*<br>Wei Xu, Ralph Grishman, Adam Meyers and Alan Ritter |
| 12:30–2:00 | Lunch |
| 2:00–2:30 | *Really? Well. Apparently Bootstrapping Improves the Performance of Sarcasm and Nastiness Classifiers for Online Dialogue*<br>Stephanie Lukin and Marilyn Walker |
| 2:30–3:00 | *Topical Positioning: A New Method for Predicting Opinion Changes in Conversation*<br>Ching-Sheng Lin, Samira Shaikh, Jennifer Stromer-Galley, Jennifer Crowley, Tomek Strzalkowski and Veena Ravishankar |
| 3:00–3:30 | *Sentiment Analysis of Political Tweets: Towards an Accurate Classifier*<br>Akshat Bakliwal, Jennifer Foster, Jennifer van der Puil, Ron O'Brien, Lamia Tounsi and Mark Hughes |
| 3:30–3:45 | Coffee Break |
| 3:45–4:15 | *A Case Study of Sockpuppet Detection in Wikipedia*<br>Thamar Solorio, Ragib Hasan and Mainul Mizan |
| 4:15–4:45 | *Towards the Detection of Reliable Food-Health Relationships*<br>Michael Wiegand and Dietrich Klakow |
| 4:45–5:15 | *Translating Government Agencies' Tweet Feeds: Specificities, Problems and (a few) Solutions*<br>Fabrizio Gotti, Philippe Langlais and Atefeh Farzindar |
| 5:15 | Closing Remarks |

# Does Size Matter?
# Text and Grammar Revision for Parsing Social Media Data

**Mohammad Khan**
Indiana University
Bloomington, IN USA
khanms@indiana.edu

**Markus Dickinson**
Indiana University
Bloomington, IN USA
md7@indiana.edu

**Sandra Kübler**
Indiana University
Bloomington, IN USA
skuebler@indiana.edu

## Abstract

We explore improving parsing social media and other web data by altering the input data, namely by normalizing web text, and by revising output parses. We find that text normalization improves performance, though spell checking has more of a mixed impact. We also find that a very simple tree reviser based on grammar comparisons performs slightly but significantly better than the baseline and well outperforms a machine learning model. The results also demonstrate that, more than the size of the training data, the goodness of fit of the data has a great impact on the parser.

## 1 Introduction and Motivation

Parsing data from social media data, as well as other data from the web, is notoriously difficult, as parsers are generally trained on news data (Petrov and McDonald, 2012), which is not a good fit for social media data. The language used in social media does not follow standard conventions (e.g., containing many sentence fragments), is largely unedited, and tends to be on different topics than standard NLP technology is trained for. At the same time, there is a clear need to develop even basic NLP technology for a variety of types of social media and contexts (e.g., Twitter, Facebook, YouTube comments, discussion forums, blogs, etc.). To perform tasks such as sentiment analysis (Nakagawa et al., 2010) or information extraction (McClosky et al., 2011), it helps to perform tagging and parsing, with an eye towards providing a shallow semantic analysis.

We advance this line of research by investigating adapting parsing to social media and other web data. Specifically, we focus on two areas: 1) We compare the impact of various text normalization techniques on parsing web data; and 2) we explore parse revision techniques for dependency parsing web data to improve the fit of the grammar learned by the parser.

One of the major problems in processing social media data is the common usage of non-standard terms (e.g., *kawaii*, a Japanese-borrowed net term for 'cute'), ungrammatical and (intentionally) misspelled text (e.g., *cuttie*), emoticons, and short posts with little contextual information, as exemplified in (1).[1]

(1) Awww cuttie little kitten, so Kawaii <3

To process such data, with its non-standard words, we first develop techniques for normalizing the text, so as to be able to accommodate the wide range of realizations of a given token, e.g., all the different spellings and intentional misspellings of *cute*. While previous research has shown the benefit of text normalization (Foster et al., 2011; Gadde et al., 2011; Foster, 2010), it has not teased apart which parts of the normalization are beneficial under which circumstances.

A second problem with parsing social media data is the data situation: parsers can be trained on the standard training set, the Penn Treebank (Marcus et al., 1993), which has a sufficient size for training a statistical parser, but has the distinct downside of modeling language that is very dissimilar

[1]Taken from: http://www.youtube.com/watch?v=eHSpHCprXLA

from the target. Or one can train parsers on the English Web Treebank (Bies et al., 2012), which covers web language, including social media data, but is rather small. Our focus on improving parsing for such data is on exploring parse revision techniques for dependency parsers. As far as we know, despite being efficient and trainable on a small amount of data, parse revision (Henestroza Anguiano and Candito, 2011; Cetinoglu et al., 2011; Attardi and Dell'Orletta, 2009; Attardi and Ciaramita, 2007) has not been used for web data, or more generally for adapting a parser to out-of-domain data; an investigation of its strengths and weaknesses is thus needed.

We describe the data sets used in our experiments in section 2 and the process of normalization in section 3 before turning to the main task of parsing in section 4. Within this section, we discuss our main parser as well as two different parse revision methods (sections 4.2 and 4.3). In the evaluation in section 5, we will find that normalization has a positive impact, although spell checking has mixed results, and that a simple tree anomaly detection method (Dickinson and Smith, 2011) outperforms a machine learning reviser (Attardi and Ciaramita, 2007), especially when integrated with confidence scores from the parser itself. In addition to the machine learner requiring a weak baseline parser, some of the main differences include the higher recall of the simple method at positing revisions and the fact that it detects odd structures, which parser confidence can then sort out as incorrect or not.

## 2 Data

For our experiments, we use two main resources, the Wall Street Journal (WSJ) portion of the Penn Treebank (PTB) (Marcus et al., 1993) and the English Web Treebank (EWT) (Bies et al., 2012). The two corpora were converted from PTB constituency trees into dependency trees using the Stanford dependency converter (de Marneffe and Manning, 2008).[2]

The EWT is comprised of approximately 16,000 sentences from weblogs, newsgroups, emails, reviews, and question-answers. Instead of examining each group individually, we chose to treat all web data equally, pulling from each type of data in the training/testing split.

```
1 <<_ -LRB--LRB-_ 2 punct _ _
2 File _ NN NN _ 0 root _ _
3 : _ : : _ 2 punct _ _
4 220b _ GW GW _ 11 dep _ _
5 -_ GW GW _ 11 dep _ _
6 dg _ GW GW _ 11 dep _ _
7 -_ GW GW _ 11 dep _ _
8 Agreement _ GW GW _ 11 dep _ _
9 for _ GW GW _ 11 dep _ _
10 Recruiting _ GW GW _ 11 dep _ _
11 Services.doc _ NN NN _ 2 dep _ _
12 >>_ -RRB--RRB-_ 2 punct _ _
13 <<_ -LRB--LRB-_ 14 punct _ _
14 File _ NN NN _ 2 dep _ _
15 : _ : : _ 14 punct _ _
16 220a _ GW GW _ 22 dep _ _
17 DG _ GW GW _ 22 dep _ _
18 -_ GW GW _ 22 dep _ _
19 Agreement _ GW GW _ 22 dep _ _
20 for _ GW GW _ 22 dep _ _
21 Contract _ GW GW _ 22 dep _ _
22 Services.DOC _ NN NN _ 14 dep _ _
23 >>_ -RRB--RRB-_ 14 punct _ _
```

Figure 1: A sentence with GW POS tags.

Additionally, for our experiments, we deleted the 212 sentences from EWT that contain the POS tags AFX and GW tags. EWT uses the POS tag AFX for cases where a prefix is written as a separate word from its root, e.g., *semi*/AFX *automatic*/JJ. Such segmentation and tagging would interfere with our normalization process. The POS tag GW is used for other non-standard words, such as document names. Such "sentences" are often difficult to analyze and do not correspond to phenomena found in the PTB (cf., figure 1).

To create training and test sets, we broke the data into the following sets:

- WSJ training: sections 02-22 (42,009 sentences)
- WSJ testing: section 23 (2,416 sentences)
- EWT training: 80% of the data, taking the first four out of every five sentences (13,130 sentences)
- EWT testing: 20% of the data, taking every fifth sentence (3,282 sentences)

[2] http://nlp.stanford.edu/software/stanford-dependencies.shtml

## 3 Text normalization

Previous work has shown that accounting for variability in form (e.g., misspellings) on the web, e.g., by mapping each form to a normalized form (Foster, 2010; Gadde et al., 2011) or by delexicalizing the parser to reduce the impact of unknown words (Øvrelid and Skjærholt, 2012), leads to some parser or tagger improvement. Foster (2010), for example, lists adapting the parser's unknown word model to handle capitalization and misspellings of function words as a possibility for improvement. Gadde et al. (2011) find that a model which posits a corrected sentence and then is POS-tagged—their tagging after correction (TAC) model—outperforms one which cleans POS tags in a postprocessing step. We follow this line of inquiry by developing text normalization techniques prior to parsing.

### 3.1 Basic text normalization

Machine learning algorithms and parsers are sensitive to the surface form of words, and different forms of a word can mislead the learner/parser. Our basic text normalization is centered around the idea that reducing unnecessary variation will lead to improved parsing performance.

For basic text normalization, we reduce all web URLs to a single token, i.e., each web URL is replaced with a uniform place-holder in the entire EWT, marking it as a URL. Similarly, all emoticons are replaced by a single marker indicating an emoticon. Repeated use of punctuation, e.g., *!!!*, is reduced to a single punctuation token.

We also have a module to shorten words with consecutive sequences of the same character: Any character that occurs more than twice in sequence will be shortened to one character, unless they appear in a dictionary, including the internet and slang dictionaries discussed below, in which case they map to the dictionary form. Thus, the word *Awww* in example (1) is shortened to *Aw*, and *cooool* maps to the dictionary form *cool*. However, since we use gold POS tags for our experiments, this module is not used in the experiments reported here.

### 3.2 Spell checking

Next, we run a spell checker to normalize misspellings, as online data often contains spelling errors (e.g. *cuttie* in example (1)). Various systems for parsing web data (e.g., from the SANCL shared task) have thus also explored spelling correction; McClosky et al. (2012), for example, used 1,057 autocorrect rules, though—since these did not make many changes—the system was not explored after that. Spell checking web data, such as YouTube comments or blog data, is a challenge because it contains non-standard orthography, as well as acronyms and other short-hand forms unknown to a standard spelling dictionary. Therefore, before mapping to a corrected spelling, it is vital to differentiate between a misspelled word and a non-standard one.

We use Aspell[3] as our spell checker to recognize and correct misspelled words. If asked to correct non-standard words, the spell checker would choose the closest standard English word, inappropriate to the context. For example, Aspell suggests *Lil* for *lol*. Thus, before correcting, we first check whether a word is an instance of *internet speech*, i.e., an abbreviation or a slang term.

We use a list of more than 3,000 acronyms to identify acronyms and other abbreviations not used commonly in formal registers of language. The list was obtained from NetLingo, restricted to the entries listed as chat acronyms and text message shorthand.[4] To identify slang terminology, we use the Urban Dictionary[5]. In a last step, we combine both lists with the list of words extracted from the WSJ.

If a word is not found in these lists, Aspell is used to suggest a correct spelling. In order to restrict Aspell from suggesting spellings that are too different from the word in question, we use Levenshtein distance (Levenshtein, 1966) to measure the degree of similarity between the original form and the suggested spelling; only words with small distances are accepted as spelling corrections. Since we have words of varying length, the Levenshtein distance is normalized by the length of the suggested spelling (i.e., number of characters). In non-exhaustive tests on a subset of the test set, we found that a normalized score of 0.301, i.e., a relatively low score accepting only conservative changes, achieves the best results when used as a threshold for accepting a sug-

[3] `www.aspell.net`
[4] `http://www.netlingo.com/acronyms.php`
[5] `www.urbandictionary.com`

gested spelling. The utilization of the threshold restricts Aspell from suggesting wrong spellings for a majority of the cases. For example, for the word *mujahidin*, Aspell suggested *Mukden*, which has a score of 1.0 and is thus rejected. Since we do not consider context or any other information besides edit distance, spell checking is not perfect and is subject to making errors, but the number of errors is considerably smaller than the number of correct revisions. For example, *lol* would be changed into *Lil* if it were not listed in the extended lexicon. Additionally, since the errors are consistent throughout the data, they result in normalization even when the spelling is wrong.

## 4 Parser revision

We use a state of the art dependency parser, MSTParser (McDonald and Pereira, 2006), as our main parser; and we use two parse revision methods: a machine learning model and a simple tree anomaly model. The goal is to be able to learn where the parser errs and to adjust the parses to be more appropriate given the target domain of social media texts.

### 4.1 Basic parser

MSTParser (McDonald and Pereira, 2006)[6] is a freely available parser which reaches state-of-the-art accuracy in dependency parsing for English. MST is a graph-based parser which optimizes its parse tree globally (McDonald et al., 2005), using a variety of feature sets, i.e., edge, sibling, context, and non-local features, employing information from words and POS tags. We use its default settings for all experiments.

We use MST as our base parser, training it in different conditions on the WSJ and the EWT. Also, MST offers the possibility to retrieve confidence scores for each dependency edge: We use the KD-Fix edge confidence scores discussed by Mejer and Crammer (2012) to assist in parse revision. As described in section 4.4, the scores are used to limit which dependencies are candidates for revision: if a dependency has a low confidence score, it may be revised, while high confidence dependencies are not considered for revision.

[6] `http://sourceforge.net/projects/mstparser/`

### 4.2 Reviser #1: machine learning model

We use DeSR (Attardi and Ciaramita, 2007) as a machine learning model of parse revision. DeSR uses a tree revision method based on decomposing revision actions into basic graph movements and learning sequences of such movements, referred to as a *revision rule*. For example, the rule `-1u` indicates that the reviser should change a dependent's head one word to the left (`-1`) and then up one element in the tree (`u`). Note that DeSR only changes the heads of dependencies, but not their labels. Such revision rules are learned for a base parser by comparing the base parser output and the gold-standard of some unseen data, based on a maximum entropy model.

In experiments, DeSR generally only considers the most frequent rules (e.g., 20), as these cover most of the errors. For best results, the reviser should: a) be trained on extra data other than the data the base parser is trained on, and b) begin with a relatively poor base parsing model. As we will see, using a fairly strong base parser presents difficulties for DeSR.

### 4.3 Reviser #2: simple tree anomaly model

Another method we use for building parse revisions is based on a method to detect anomalies in parse structures (APS) using $n$-gram sequences of dependency structures (Dickinson and Smith, 2011; Dickinson, 2010). The method checks whether the same head category (e.g., verb) has a set of dependents similar to others of the same category (Dickinson, 2010).

To see this, consider the partial tree in figure 2, from the dependency-converted EWT.[7] This tree is converted to a rule as in (2), where all dependents of a head are realized.

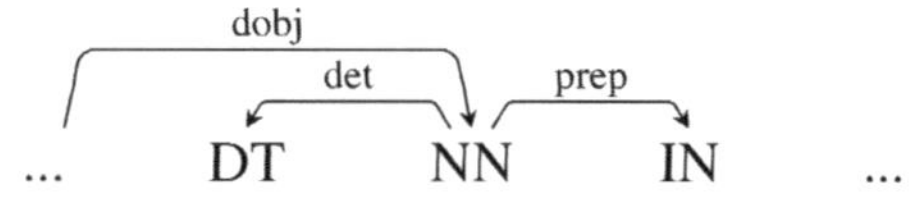


Figure 2: A sketch of a basic dependency tree

(2) dobj → det:DT NN **prep:IN**

[7] DT/det=determiner, NN=noun, IN/prep=preposition, dobj=direct object

This rule is then broken down into its component $n$-grams and compared to other rules, using the formula for scoring an element ($e_i$) in (3). $N$-gram counts ($C(ngrm)$) come from a training corpus; an instantiation for this rule is in (4).

(3) $s(e_i) = \sum_{ngrm: e_i \in ngrm \wedge n \geq 3} C(ngrm)$

(4) $s$(prep:IN) = $C$(det:DT NN **prep:IN**)
+ $C$(NN **prep:IN** END)
+ $C$(START det:DT NN **prep:IN**)
+ $C$(det:DT NN **prep:IN** END)
+ $C$(START det:DT NN **prep:IN** END)

We modify the scoring slightly, incorporating bigrams ($n \geq 2$), but weighing them as 0.01 of a count ($C(ngrm)$); this handles the issue that bigrams are not very informative, yet having some bigrams is better than none (Dickinson and Smith, 2011).

The method detects non-standard parses which may result from parser error or because the text is unusual in some other way, e.g., ungrammatical (Dickinson, 2011). The structures deemed atypical depend upon the corpus used for obtaining the grammar that parser output is compared to.

With a method of scoring the quality of individual dependents in a tree, one can compare the score of a dependent to the score obtaining by hypothesizing a revision. For error detection, this ameliorates the effect of odd structures for which no better parse is available. The revision checking algorithm in Dickinson and Smith (2011) posits new labelings and attachments—maintaining projectivity and acyclicity, to consider only reasonable candidates[8]—and checks whether any have a higher score.[9] If so, the token is flagged as having a better revision and is more likely to be an error.

In other words, the method checks revisions for error detection. With a simple modification of the code,[10] one can also keep track of the best revision for each token and actually change the tree structure. This is precisely what we do. Because the method relies upon very coarse scores, it can suggest too many revisions; in tandem with parser confidence, though, this can filter the set of revisions to a reasonable amount, as discussed next.

### 4.4 Pinpointing erroneous parses

The parse revision methods rely both on being able to detect errors and on being able to correct them. We can assist the methods by using MST confidence scores (Mejer and Crammer, 2012) to pinpoint candidates for revision, and only pass these candidates on to the parse revisers. For example, since APS (anomaly detection) detects atypical structures (section 4.3), some of which may not be errors, it will find many strange parses and revise many positions on its own, though some be questionable revisions. By using a confidence filter, though, we only consider ones flagged below a certain MST confidence score. We follow Mejer and Crammer (2012) and use confidence$\leq$0.5 as our threshold for identifying errors. Non-exhaustive tests on a subset of the test set show good performance with this threshold.

In the experiments reported in section 5, if we use the revision methods to revise everything, we refer to this as the *DeSR* and the *APS* models; if we filter out high confidence cases and restrict revisions to low confidence scoring cases, we refer to this as *DeSR restricted* and *APS restricted*.

Before using the MST confidence scores as part of the revision process, then, we first report on using the scores for error detection at the $\leq$0.5 threshold, as shown in table 1. As we can see, using confidence scores allows us to pinpoint errors with high precision. With a recall around 40–50%, we find errors with upwards of 90% precision, meaning that these cases are in need of revision. Interestingly, the highest error detection precision comes with WSJ as part of the training data and EWT as the testing. This could be related to the great difference between the WSJ and EWT grammatical models and the greater number of unknown words in this experiment, though more investigation is needed. Although data sets are hard to compare, the precision seems to outperform that of more generic (i.e., non-parser-specific) error detection methods (Dickinson and Smith, 2011).

[8] We remove the cyclicity check, in order to be able to detect errors where the head and dependent are flipped.

[9] We actually check whether a new score is greater than or equal to twice the original score, to account for meaningless differences for large values, e.g., 1001 vs. 1000. We do not expect our minor modifications to have a huge impact, though more robust testing is surely required.

[10] `http://cl.indiana.edu/~md7/papers/dickinson-smith11.html`

| Train | Test | Normalization (on test) | Tokens | Attach. Errors | Label. Errors | Total Errors | Precision | Recall |
|---|---|---|---|---|---|---|---|---|
| WSJ | WSJ | none | 4,621 | 2,452 | 1,297 | 3,749 | 0.81 | 0.40 |
| WSJ | EWT | none | 5,855 | 3,621 | 2,169 | 5,790 | 0.99 | 0.38 |
| WSJ | EWT | full | 5,617 | 3,484 | 1,959 | 5,443 | 0.97 | 0.37 |
| EWT | EWT | none | 7,268 | 4,083 | 2,202 | 6,285 | 0.86 | 0.51 |
| EWT | EWT | full | 7,131 | 3,905 | 2,147 | 6,052 | 0.85 | 0.50 |
| WSJ+EWT | EWT | none | 5,622 | 3,338 | 1,849 | 5,187 | 0.92 | 0.40 |
| WSJ+EWT | EWT | full | 5,640 | 3,379 | 1,862 | 5,241 | 0.93 | 0.41 |

Table 1: Error detection results for MST confidence scores ($\leq 0.5$) for different conditions and normalization settings. Number of tokens and errors below the threshold are reported.

## 5 Experiments

We report three major sets of experiments: the first set compares the two parse revision strategies; the second looks into text normalization strategies; and the third set investigates whether the size of the training set or its similarity to the target domain is more important. Since we are interested in parsing in these experiments, we use gold POS tags as input for the parser, in order to exclude any unwanted interaction between POS tagging and parsing.

### 5.1 Parser revision

In this experiment, we are interested in comparing a machine learning method to a simple $n$-gram revision model. For all experiments, we use the original version of the EWT data, without any normalization.

The results of this set of experiments are shown in table 2. The first row reports MST's performance on the standard WSJ data split, giving an idea of an upper bound for these experiments. The second part shows MST's performance on the EWT data, when trained on WSJ or the combination of the WSJ and EWT training sets. Note that there is considerable decrease for both settings in terms of *unlabeled accuracy* (UAS) and *labeled accuracy* (LAS), of approximately 8% when trained on WSJ and 5.5% on WSJ+EWT. This drop in score is consistent with previous work on non-canonical data, e.g., web data (Foster et al., 2011) and learner language (Krivanek and Meurers, 2011). It is difficult to compare these results, due to different training and testing conditions, but MST (without any modifications) reaches results that are in the mid-high range of results reported by Petrov and McDonald (2012, table 4) in their overview of the SANCL shared task using the EWT data: 80.10–87.62% UAS; 71.04%–83.46% LAS.

Next, we look at the performance of the two revisers on the same data sets. Note that since DeSR requires training data for the revision part that is different from the training set of the base parser, we conduct parsing and revision in DeSR with two different data sets. Thus, for the WSJ experiment, we split the WSJ training set into two parts, WSJ02-11 and WSJ12-2, instead of training on the whole WSJ. For the EWT training set, we split this set into two parts and use 25% of it for training the parser (EWTs) and the rest for training the reviser (EWTr). In contrast, APS does not need extra data for training and thus was trained on the same data as the base parser. While this means that the base parser for DeSR has a smaller training set, note that DeSR works best with a weak base parser (Attardi, p.c.).

The results show that DeSR's performance is below MST's on the same data. In other words, adding DeSRs revisions decreases accuracy. APS also shows a deterioration in the results, but the difference is much smaller. Also, training on a combination of WSJ and EWT data increases the performance of both revisers by 2-3% over training solely on WSJ.

Since these results show that the revisions are harmful, we decided to restrict the revisions further by using MST's KD-Fix edge confidence scores, as described in section 4.4. We apply the revisions only if MST's confidence in this dependency is low (i.e., below or equal to 0.5). The results of this experiment are shown in the last section of table 2. We can see

| Method | Parser Train | Reviser Train | Test | UAS | LAS |
|---|---|---|---|---|---|
| MST | WSJ | n/a | WSJ | 89.94 | 87.24 |
| MST | WSJ | n/a | EWT | 81.98 | 78.65 |
| MST | WSJ+EWT | n/a | EWT | 84.50 | 81.61 |
| DeSR | WSJ02-11 | WSJ12-22 | EWT | 80.63 | 77.33 |
| DeSR | WSJ+EWTs | EWTr | EWT | 82.68 | 79.77 |
| APS | WSJ | WSJ | EWT | 81.96 | 78.40 |
| APS | WSJ+EWT | WSJ+EWT | EWT | 84.45 | 81.29 |
| DeSR restricted | WSJ+EWTs | EWTr | EWT | 84.40 | 81.50 |
| APS restricted | WSJ+EWT | WSJ+EWT | EWT | ***84.53*** | ****81.66*** |

Table 2: Results of comparing a machine learning reviser (DeSR) with a tree anomaly model (APS), with base parser MST (* = sig. at the 0.05 level, as compared to row 2).

that both revisers improve over their non-restricted versions. However, while DeSR's results are still below MST's baseline results, APS shows slight improvements over the MST baseline, significant in the LAS. Significance was tested using the CoNLL-X evaluation script in combination with Dan Bikel's Randomized Parsing Evaluation Comparator, which is based on sampling.[11]

For the original experiment, APS changes 1,402 labels and 272 attachments of the MST output. In the restricted version, label changes are reduced to 610, and attachment to 167. In contrast, DeSR changes 1,509 attachments but only 303 in the restricted version. The small numbers, given that we have more than 3,000 sentences in the test set, show that finding reliable revisions is a difficult task. Since both revisers are used more or less off the shelf, there is much room to improve.

Based on these results and other results based on different settings, which, for DeSR, resulted in low accuracy, we decided to concentrate on APS in the following experiments, and more specifically focus on the restricted version of APS to see whether there are significant improvements under different data conditions.

### 5.2 Text normalization

In this set of experiments, we investigate the influence of the text normalization strategies presented in section 3 on parsing and more specifically on our parse revision strategy. Thus, we first apply a *partial normalization*, using only the basic text normalization. For the *full normalization*, we combine the basic text normalization with the spell checker. For these experiments, we use the restricted APS reviser and the EWT treebank for training and testing.

The results are shown in table 3. Note that since we also normalize the training set, MST will also profit from the normalizations. For this reason, we present MST and APS (restricted) results for each type of normalization. The first part of the table shows the results for MST and APS without any normalization; the numbers here are higher than in table 2 because we now train only on EWT—an issue we take up in section 5.3. The second part shows the results for partial normalization. These results show that both approaches profit from the normalization to the same degree: both UAS and LAS increase by approximately 0.25 percent points. When we look at the full normalization, including spell checking, we can see that it does not have a positive effect on MST but that APS's results increase, especially unlabeled accuracy. Note that all APS versions significantly outperform the MST versions but also that both normalized MST versions significantly outperform the non-normalized MST.

### 5.3 WSJ versus domain data

In these experiments, we are interested in which type of training data allows us to reach the highest accuracy in parsing. Is it more useful to use a large, out-of-domain training set (WSJ in our case), a small, in-domain training set, or a combination of both? Our assumption was that the largest data set, consisting of the WSJ and the EWT training sets, would

[11] `http://ilk.uvt.nl/conll/software.html`

| Norm. | Method | UAS | LAS |
|---|---|---|---|
| Train:no; Test:no | MST | 84.87 | 82.21 |
| Train:no; Test:no | APS restr. | *******84.90* | ***82.23* |
| Train:part; Test:part | MST | *85.12 | *82.45 |
| Train:part; Test:part | APS restr. | ***85.18* | **82.50* |
| Train:full; Test:full | MST | **85.20 | *82.45 |
| Train:full; Test:full | APS restr. | *****85.24*** | *****82.52*** |

Table 3: Results of comparing different types of text normalization, training and testing on EWT sets. (Significance tested for APS versions as compared to the corresponding MST version and for each MST with the non-normalized MST: * = sig. at the 0.05 level, ** = significance at the 0.01 level).

give the best results. For these experiments, we use the EWT test set and different combinations of text normalization, and the results are shown in table 4.

The first three sections in the table show the results of training on the WSJ and testing on the EWT. The results show that both MST and APS profit from text normalization. Surprisingly, the best results are gained by using the partial normalization; adding the spell checker (for full normalization) is detrimental, because the spell checker introduces additional errors that result in extra, non-standard words in EWT. Such additional variation in words is not present in the original training model of the base parser.

For the experiments with the EWT and the combined WSJ+EWT training sets, spell checking does help, and we report only the results with full normalization since this setting gave us the best results. To our surprise, results with only the EWT as training set surpass those of using the full WSJ+EWT training sets (a UAS of 85.24% and a LAS of 82.52% for EWT vs. a UAS of 82.34% and a LAS of 79.31%). Note, however, that when we reduce the size of the WSJ data such that it matches the size of the EWT data, performance increases to the highest results, a UAS of 86.41% and a LAS of 83.67%. Taken together, these results seem to indicate that quality (i.e., in-domain data) is more important than mere (out-of-domain) quantity, but also that more out-of-domain data can help if it does not overwhelm the in-domain data. It is also obvious that MST per se profits the most from normalization, but that the APS consistently provides small but significant improvements over the MST baseline.

## 6 Summary and Outlook

We examined ways to improve parsing social media and other web data by altering the input data, namely by normalizing such texts, and by revising output parses. We found that normalization improves performance, though spell checking has more of a mixed impact. We also found that a very simple tree reviser based on grammar comparisons performs slightly but significantly better than the baseline, across different experimental conditions, and well outperforms a machine learning model. The results also demonstrated that, more than the size of the training data, the goodness of fit of the data has a great impact on the parser. Perhaps surprisingly, adding the entire WSJ training data to web training data leads to a deteriment in performance, whereas balancing it with web data has the best performance.

There are many ways to take this work in the future. The small, significant improvements from the APS restricted reviser indicate that there is potential for improvement in pursuing such grammar-corrective models for parse revision. The model we use relies on a simplistic notion of revisions, neither checking the resulting well-formedness of the tree nor how one correction influences other corrections. One could also, for example, treat grammars from different domains in different ways to improve scoring and revision. Another possibility would be to apply the parse revisions also to the out-of-domain training data, to make it more similar to the in-domain data.

For text normalization, the module could benefit from a few different improvements. For example, non-contracted words such as *well* to mean *we'll* require a more complicated normalization step, in-

| Train | Test | Normalization | Method | UAS | LAS |
|---|---|---|---|---|---|
| WSJ | EWT | train:no; test:no | MST | 81.98 | 78.65 |
| WSJ | EWT | train:no; test:no | APS | 81.96 | 78.40 |
| WSJ | EWT | train:no; test:no | APS restr | *82.02* | ***78.71* |
| WSJ | EWT | train:no; test:part | MST | 82.31 | 79.27 |
| WSJ | EWT | train:no; test:part | APS restr. | **82.36* | **79.32* |
| WSJ | EWT | train:no; test:full | MST | 82.30 | 79.26 |
| WSJ | EWT | train:no; test:full | APS restr. | *82.34* | **79.31* |
| EWT | EWT | train:full; test:full | MST | 85.20 | 82.45 |
| EWT | EWT | train:full; test:full | APS restr. | ***85.24* | ***82.52* |
| WSJ+EWT | EWT | train:full; test:full | MST | 84.59 | 81.68 |
| WSJ+EWT | EWT | train:full; test:full | APS restr. | ***84.63* | **81.73* |
| Balanced WSJ+EWT | EWT | train:full; test:full | MST | 86.38 | 83.62 |
| Balanced WSJ+EWT | EWT | train:full; test:full | APS restr. | ****86.41*** | *****83.67*** |

Table 4: Results of different training data sets and normalization patterns on parsing the EWT test data. (Significance tested for APS versions as compared to the corresponding MST: * = sig. at the 0.05 level, ** = sig. at the 0.01 level)

volving machine learning or $n$-gram language models. In general, language models could be used for more context-sensitive spelling correction. Given the preponderance of terms on the web, using a named entity recognizer (e.g., Finkel et al., 2005) for preprocessing may also provide benefits.

## Acknowledgments

We would like to thank Giuseppe Attardi for his help in using DeSR; Can Liu, Shoshana Berleant, and the IU CL discussion group for discussion; and the three anonymous reviewers for their helpful comments.

## References

Giuseppe Attardi and Massimiliano Ciaramita. 2007. Tree revision learning for dependency parsing. In *Proceedings of HLT-NAACL-07*, pages 388–395. Rochester, NY.

Giuseppe Attardi and Felice Dell'Orletta. 2009. Reverse revision and linear tree combination for dependency parsing. In *Proceedings of HLT-NAACL-09, Short Papers*, pages 261–264. Boulder, CO.

Ann Bies, Justin Mott, Colin Warner, and Seth Kulick. 2012. English Web Treebank. Linguistic Data Consortium, Philadelphia, PA.

Ozlem Cetinoglu, Anton Bryl, Jennifer Foster, and Josef Van Genabith. 2011. Improving dependency label accuracy using statistical post-editing: A cross-framework study. In *Proceedings of the International Conference on Dependency Linguistics*, pages 300–309. Barcelona, Spain.

Marie-Catherine de Marneffe and Christopher D. Manning. 2008. The Stanford typed dependencies representation. In *COLING 2008 Workshop on Cross-framework and Cross-domain Parser Evaluation*. Manchester, England.

Markus Dickinson. 2010. Detecting errors in automatically-parsed dependency relations. In *Proceedings of ACL-10*. Uppsala, Sweden.

Markus Dickinson. 2011. Detecting ad hoc rules for treebank development. *Linguistic Issues in Language Technology*, 4(3).

Markus Dickinson and Amber Smith. 2011. Detecting dependency parse errors with minimal resources. In *Proceedings of IWPT-11*, pages 241–252. Dublin, Ireland.

Jenny Rose Finkel, Trond Grenager, and Christopher Manning. 2005. Incorporating non-local information into information extraction systems by gibbs sampling. In *Proceedings of ACL'05*, pages 363–370. Ann Arbor, MI.

Jennifer Foster. 2010. "cba to check the spelling": Investigating parser performance on discussion forum posts. In *Proceedings of NAACL-HLT 2010*, pages 381–384. Los Angeles, CA.

Jennifer Foster, Ozlem Cetinoglu, Joachim Wagner, Joseph Le Roux, Joakim Nivre, Deirdre Hogan, and Josef van Genabith. 2011. From news to comment: Resources and benchmarks for parsing the language of web 2.0. In *Proceedings of IJCNLP-11*, pages 893–901. Chiang Mai, Thailand.

Phani Gadde, L. V. Subramaniam, and Tanveer A. Faruquie. 2011. Adapting a WSJ trained part-of-speech tagger to noisy text: Preliminary results. In *Proceedings of Joint Workshop on Multilingual OCR and Analytics for Noisy Unstructured Text Data*. Beijing, China.

Enrique Henestroza Anguiano and Marie Candito. 2011. Parse correction with specialized models for difficult attachment types. In *Proceedings of EMNLP-11*, pages 1222–1233. Edinburgh, UK.

Julia Krivanek and Detmar Meurers. 2011. Comparing rule-based and data-driven dependency parsing of learner language. In *Proceedings of the Int. Conference on Dependency Linguistics (Depling 2011)*, pages 310–317. Barcelona.

Vladimir I. Levenshtein. 1966. Binary codes capable of correcting deletions, insertions, and reversals. *Cybernetics and Control Theory*, 10(8):707–710.

Mitchell Marcus, Beatrice Santorini, and Mary Ann Marcinkiewicz. 1993. Building a large annotated corpus of English: The Penn Treebank. *Computational Linguistics*, 19(2):313–330.

David McClosky, Wanxiang Che, Marta Recasens, Mengqiu Wang, Richard Socher, and Christopher Manning. 2012. Stanford's system for parsing the English web. In *Workshop on the Syntactic Analysis of Non-Canonical Language (SANCL 2012)*. Montreal, Canada.

David McClosky, Mihai Surdeanu, and Christopher Manning. 2011. Event extraction as dependency parsing. In *Proceedings of ACL-HLT-11*, pages 1626–1635. Portland, OR.

Ryan McDonald, Koby Crammer, and Fernando Pereira. 2005. Online large-margin training of dependency parsers. In *Proceedings of ACL-05*, pages 91–98. Ann Arbor, MI.

Ryan McDonald and Fernando Pereira. 2006. Online learning of approximate dependency parsing algorithms. In *Proceedings of EACL-06*. Trento, Italy.

Avihai Mejer and Koby Crammer. 2012. Are you sure? Confidence in prediction of dependency tree edges. In *Proceedings of the NAACL-HTL 2012*, pages 573–576. Montréal, Canada.

Tetsuji Nakagawa, Kentaro Inui, and Sadao Kurohashi. 2010. Dependency tree-based sentiment classification using CRFs with hidden variables. In *Proceedings of NAACL-HLT 2010*, pages 786–794. Los Angeles, CA.

Lilja Øvrelid and Arne Skjærholt. 2012. Lexical categories for improved parsing of web data. In *Proceedings of the 24th International Conference on Computational Linguistics (COLING 2012)*, pages 903–912. Mumbai, India.

Slav Petrov and Ryan McDonald. 2012. Overview of the 2012 shared task on parsing the web. In *Workshop on the Syntactic Analysis of Non-Canonical Language (SANCL 2012)*. Montreal, Canada.

# Phonological Factors in Social Media Writing

**Jacob Eisenstein**
jacobe@gatech.edu
School of Interactive Computing
Georgia Institute of Technology

## Abstract

Does phonological variation get transcribed into social media text? This paper investigates examples of the phonological variable of consonant cluster reduction in Twitter. Not only does this variable appear frequently, but it displays the same sensitivity to linguistic context as in spoken language. This suggests that when social media writing transcribes phonological properties of speech, it is not merely a case of inventing orthographic transcriptions. Rather, social media displays influence from structural properties of the phonological system.

## 1 Introduction

The differences between social media text and other forms of written language are a subject of increasing interest for both language technology (Gimpel et al., 2011; Ritter et al., 2011; Foster et al., 2011) and linguistics (Androutsopoulos, 2011; Dresner and Herring, 2010; Paolillo, 1996). Many words that are endogenous to social media have been linked with specific geographical regions (Eisenstein et al., 2010; Wing and Baldridge, 2011) and demographic groups (Argamon et al., 2007; Rao et al., 2010; Eisenstein et al., 2011), raising the question of whether this variation is related to spoken language dialects. Dialect variation encompasses differences at multiple linguistic levels, including the lexicon, morphology, syntax, and phonology. While previous work on group differences in social media language has generally focused on lexical differences, this paper considers the most purely "spoken" aspect of dialect: phonology.

Specifically, this paper presents evidence against the following two null hypotheses:

- H0: Phonological variation does not impact social media text.
- H1: Phonological variation may introduce new lexical items into social media text, but not the underlying structural rules.

These hypotheses are examined in the context of the phonological variable of *consonant cluster reduction* (also known as consonant cluster simplification, or more specifically, -/t,d/ deletion). When a word ends in cluster of consonant sounds — for example, *mist* or *missed* — the cluster may be simplified, for example, to *miss*. This well-studied variable has been demonstrated in a number of different English dialects, including African American English (Labov et al., 1968; Green, 2002), Tejano and Chicano English (Bayley, 1994; Santa Ana, 1991), and British English (Tagliamonte and Temple, 2005); it has also been identified in other languages, such as Quebecois French (Côté, 2004). While some previous work has cast doubt on the influence of spoken dialects on written language (Whiteman, 1982; Thompson et al., 2004), this paper presents large-scale evidence for consonant cluster reduction in social media text from Twitter — in contradiction of the null hypothesis H0.

But even if social media authors introduce new orthographic *transcriptions* to capture the sound of language in the dialect that they speak, such innovations may be purely lexical. Phonological variation is governed by a network of interacting preferences that include the surrounding linguistic context. Do these structural aspects of phonological variation also appear in written social media?

Consonant cluster reduction is a classic example of the complex workings of phonological variation: its frequency depends on the morphology of the word in which it appears, as well as the phonology of the preceding and subsequent segments. The variable is therefore a standard test case for models of the interaction between phonological preferences (Guy, 1991). For our purposes, the key point is that consonant cluster reduction is strongly inhibited when the subsequent phonological segment begins with a vowel. The final *t* in *left* is more likely to be deleted in *I left* ***the*** *house* than in *I left* ***a*** *tip*. Guy (1991) writes, "prior studies are unanimous that a following consonant promotes deletion more readily than a following vowel," and more recent work continues to uphold this finding (Tagliamonte and Temple, 2005).

Consonant cluster reduction thus provides an opportunity to test the null hypothesis H1. If the introduction of phonological variation into social media writing occurs only on the level of new lexical items, that would predict that reduced consonant clusters would be followed by consonant-initial and vowel-initial segments at roughly equal rates. But if consonant cluster reduction is inhibited by adjacent vowel-initial segments in social media text, that would argue against H1. The experiments in this paper provide evidence of such context-sensitivity, suggesting that the influence of phonological variation on social media text must be deeper than the transcription of invidual lexical items.

## 2 Word pairs

The following word pairs were considered:

- *left / lef*
- *just / jus*
- *with / wit*
- *going / goin*
- *doing / doin*
- *know / kno*

The first two pairs display consonant cluster reduction, specifically t-deletion. As mentioned above, consonant cluster reduction is a property of African American English (AAE) and several other English dialects. The pair *with/wit* represents a stopping of the interdental fricative, a characteristic of New York English (Gordon, 2004), rural Southern English (Thomas, 2004), as well as AAE (Green, 2002). The next two pairs represent "g-dropping", the replacement of the velar nasal with the coronal nasal, which has been associated with informal speech in many parts of the English-speaking world.[1] The final word pair *know/kno* does not differ in pronunciation, and is included as a control.

These pairs were selected because they are all frequently-used words, and because they cover a range of typical "shortenings" in social media and other computer mediated communication (Gouws et al., 2011). Another criterion is that each shortened form can be recognized relatively unambiguously. Although *wit* and *wan* are standard English words, close examination of the data did not reveal any examples in which the surface forms could be construed to indicate these words. Other words were rejected for this reason: for example, *best* may be reduced to *bes*, but this surface form is frequently used as an acronym for *Blackberry Enterprise Server*.

Consonant cluster reduction may be combined with morphosyntactic variation, particularly in African American English. Thompson et al. (2004) describe several such cases: zero past tense (*mother kiss(ed) them all goodbye*), zero plural (*the children made their bed(s)*), and subject-verb agreement (*then she jump(s) on the roof*). In each of these cases, it is unclear whether it is the morphosyntactic or phonological process that is responsible for the absence of the final consonant. Words that feature such ambiguity, such as *past*, were avoided.

Table 1 shows five randomly sampled examples of each shortened form. Only the relevant portion of each message is shown. From consideration of many examples such as these, it is clear that the shortened forms *lef, jus, wit, goin, doin, kno* refer to the standard forms *left, just, with, going, doing, know* in the overwhelming majority of cases.

[1] Language Log offers an engaging discussion of the linguistic and cultural history of "g-dropping." `http://itre.cis.upenn.edu/~myl/languagelog/archives/000878.html`

1. *ok* ***lef*** *the y had a good workout*
   (ok, left the YMCA, had a good workout)
2. *@USER* ***lef*** *the house*
3. *eat off d wol a d rice and* ***lef*** *d meat*
   (... left the meat)
4. *she nah* ***lef*** *me*
   (she has not left me)
5. *i* ***lef*** *my changer*

6. ***jus*** *livin this thing called life*
7. *all the money he* ***jus*** *took out the bank*
8. *boutta* ***jus*** *strt tweatin random shxt*
   (about to just start tweeting ...)
9. *i* ***jus*** *look at shit way different*
10. *u* ***jus*** *fuckn lamee*

11. *fall in love* ***wit*** *her*
12. *i mess* ***wit*** *pockets*
13. *da hell* ***wit*** *u*
    (the hell with you)
14. *drinks* ***wit*** *my bro*
15. *don't fuck* ***wit*** *him*

16. *a team that's* ***goin*** *to continue*
17. *what's* ***goin*** *on tonight*
18. *is reign stil* ***goin*** *down*
19. *when is she* ***goin*** *bck 2 work?*
20. *ur not* ***goin*** *now where*
    (you're not going nowhere)

21. *u were* ***doin*** *the same thing*
22. *he* ***doin*** *big things*
23. *i'm not* ***doin*** *shit this weekend*
24. *oh u* ***doin*** *it for haiti huh*
25. *i damn sure aint* ***doin*** *it in the am*

26. *u* ***kno*** *u gotta put up pics*
27. *i* ***kno*** *some people bout to be sick*
28. *u already* ***kno***
29. *you* ***kno*** *im not ugly pendeja*
30. *now i* ***kno*** *why i'm always on netflix*

Table 1: examples of each shortened form

## 3 Data

Our research is supported by a dataset of microblog posts from the social media service Twitter. This service allows its users to post 140-character messages. Each author's messages appear in the newsfeeds of individuals who have chosen to "follow" the author, though by default the messages are publicly available to anyone on the Internet. Twitter has relatively broad penetration across different ethnicities, genders, and income levels. The Pew Research Center has repeatedly polled the demographics of Twitter (Smith and Brewer, 2012), finding: nearly identical usage among women (15% of female internet users are on Twitter) and men (14%); high usage among non-Hispanic Blacks (28%); an even distribution across income and education levels; higher usage among young adults (26% for ages 18-29, 4% for ages 65+).

Twitter's streaming API delivers an ongoing random sample of messages from the complete set of public messages on the service. The data in this study was gathered from the public "Gardenhose" feed, which is claimed to be approximately 10% of all public posts; however, recent research suggests that the sampling rate for geolocated posts is much higher (Morstatter et al., 2013). This data was gathered over a period from August 2009 through the end of September 2012, resulting in a total of 114 million messages from 2.77 million different user accounts (Eisenstein et al., 2012).

Several filters were applied to ensure that the dataset is appropriate for the research goals of this paper. The dataset includes only messages that contain geolocation metadata, which is optionally provided by smartphone clients. Each message must have a latitude and longitude within a United States census block, which enables the demographic analysis in Section 6. Retweets are excluded (both as identified in the official Twitter API, as well as messages whose text includes the token "RT"), as are messages that contain a URL. Grouping tweets by author, we retain only authors who have fewer than 1000 "followers" (people who have chosen to view the author's messages in their newsfeed) and who follow fewer than 1000 individuals.

Specific instances of the word pairs are acquired by using `grep` to identify messages in which the shortened form is followed by another sequence of purely alphabetic characters. Reservoir sampling (Vitter, 1985) was used to obtain a randomized set of at most 10,000 messages for each word. There were only 753 examples of the shortening *lef*; for all other words we obtain the full 10,000 messages. For each shortened word, an equal number of samples for the standard form were obtained through the same method: `grep` piped through a reservoir sampler. Each instance of the standard form must also be followed by a purely alphabetic string. Note that the total number of instances is slightly higher than the number of messages, because a word may appear multiple times within the same message. The counts are shown in Table 2.

## 4 Analysis 1: Frequency of vowels after word shortening

The first experiment tests the hypothesis that consonant clusters are less likely to be reduced when followed by a word that begins with a vowel letter. Table 2 presents the counts for each term, along with the probability that the next segment begins with the vowel. The probabilities are accompanied by 95% confidence intervals, which are computed from the standard deviation of the binomial distribution.All differences are statistically significant at $p < .05$.

The simplified form *lef* is followed by a vowel only 19% of the time, while the complete form *left* is followed by a vowel 35% of the time. The absolute difference for *jus* and *just* is much smaller, but with such large counts, even this 2% absolute difference is unlikely to be a chance fluctuation.

The remaining results are more mixed. The shortened form *wit* is significantly *more* likely to be followed by a vowel than its standard form *with*. The two "g dropping" examples are inconsistent, and troublingly, there is a significant effect in the control condition. For these reasons, a more fine-grained analysis is pursued in the next section.

A potential complication to these results is that cluster reduction may be especially likely in specific phrases. For example, *most* can be reduced to *mos*, but in a sample of 1000 instances of this reduction, 72% occurred within a single expression: *mos def*. This phrase can be either an expression of certainty (*most definitely*), or a reference to the performing artist of the same name. If *mos* were observed to

| word | $N$ | $N$(vowel) | P(vowel) |
|---|---|---|---|
| *lef* | 753 | 145 | $0.193 \pm 0.028$ |
| *left* | 757 | 265 | $0.350 \pm 0.034$ |
| *jus* | 10336 | 939 | $0.091 \pm 0.006$ |
| *just* | 10411 | 1158 | $0.111 \pm 0.006$ |
| *wit* | 10405 | 2513 | $0.242 \pm 0.008$ |
| *with* | 10510 | 2328 | $0.222 \pm 0.008$ |
| *doin* | 10203 | 2594 | $0.254 \pm 0.008$ |
| *doing* | 10198 | 2793 | $0.274 \pm 0.009$ |
| *goin* | 10197 | 3194 | $0.313 \pm 0.009$ |
| *going* | 10275 | 1821 | $0.177 \pm 0.007$ |
| *kno* | 10387 | 3542 | $0.341 \pm 0.009$ |
| *know* | 10402 | 3070 | $0.295 \pm 0.009$ |

Table 2: Term counts and probability with which the following segment begins with a vowel. All differences are significant at $p < .05$.

be more likely to be followed by a consonant-initial word than *most*, this might be attributable to this one expression.

An inverse effect could explain the high likelihood that *goin* is followed by a vowel. Given that the author has chosen an informal register, the phrase *goin to* is likely to be replaced by *gonna*. One might hypothesize the following decision tree:

- If formal register, use *going*
- If informal register,
  - If next word is *to*, use *gonna*
  - else, use *goin*

Counts for each possibility are shown in Table 3; these counts are drawn from a subset of the 100,000 messages and thus cannot be compared directly with Table 2. Nonetheless, since *to* is by far the most frequent successor to *going*, a great deal of *going*'s preference for consonant successors can be explained by the word *to*.

## 5 Analysis 2: Logistic regression to control for lexical confounds

While it is tempting to simply remove *going to* and *goin to* from the dataset, this would put us on a slippery slope: where do we draw the line between lexical confounds and phonological effects? Rather than

| | total | ... *to* | percentage |
|---|---|---|---|
| *going* | 1471 | 784 | 53.3% |
| *goin* | 470 | 107 | 22.8% |
| *gonna* | 1046 | n/a | n/a |

Table 3: Counts for *going to* and related phrases in the first 100,000 messages in the dataset. The shortened form *goin* is far less likely to be followed by *to*, possibly because of the frequently-chosen *gonna* alternative.

| word | $\mu_\beta$ | $\sigma_\beta$ | $z$ | $p$ |
|---|---|---|---|---|
| *lef/left* | -0.45 | 0.10 | -4.47 | $3.9 \times 10^{-6}$ |
| *jus/just* | -0.43 | 0.11 | -3.98 | $3.4 \times 10^{-5}$ |
| *wit/with* | -0.16 | 0.03 | -4.96 | $3.6 \times 10^{-7}$ |
| *doin/doing* | 0.08 | 0.04 | 2.29 | 0.011 |
| *goin/going* | -0.07 | 0.05 | -1.62 | 0.053 |
| *kno/know* | -0.07 | 0.05 | -1.23 | 0.11 |

Table 4: Logistic regression coefficients for the VOWEL feature, predicting the choice of the shortened form. Negative values indicate that the shortened form is less likely if followed by a vowel, when controlling for lexical features.

excluding such examples from the dataset, it would be preferable to apply analytic techniques capable of sorting out lexical and systematic effects. One such technique is logistic regression, which forces lexical and phonological factors to **compete** for the right to explain the observed orthographic variations.[2]

The dependent variable indicates whether the word-final consonant cluster was reduced. The independent variables include a single feature indicating whether the successor word begins with a vowel, and additional lexical features for all possible successor words. If the orthographic variation is best explained by a small number of successor words, the phonological VOWEL feature will not acquire significant weight.

Table 4 presents the mean and standard deviation of the logistic regression coefficient for the VOWEL feature, computed over 1000 bootstrapping iterations (Wasserman, 2005).[3] The coefficient has the largest magnitude in cases of consonant cluster reduction, and the associated p-values indicate strong statistical significance. The VOWEL coefficient is also strongly significant for *wit/with*. It reaches the $p < .05$ threshold for *doin/doing*, although in this case, the presence of a vowel indicates a preference for the shortened form *doin* — contra the raw frequencies in Table 2. The coefficient for the VOWEL feature is not significantly different from zero for *goin/going* and for the control *kno/know*. Note that since we had no prior expectation of the coefficient sign in these cases, a two-tailed test would be most appropriate, with critical value $\alpha = 0.025$ to establish 95% confidence.

## 6 Analysis 3: Social variables

The final analysis concerns the relationship between phonological variation and social variables. In spoken language, the word pairs chosen in this study have connections with both ethnic and regional dialects: consonant cluster reduction is a feature of African-American English (Green, 2002) and Tejano and Chicano English (Bayley, 1994; Santa Ana, 1991); th-stopping (as in *wit/with*) is a feature of African-American English (Green, 2002) as well as several regional dialects (Gordon, 2004; Thomas, 2004); the velar nasal in *doin* and *goin* is a property of informal speech. The control pair *kno/know* does not correspond to any sound difference, and thus there is no prior evidence about its relationship to social variables.

The dataset includes the average latitude and longitude for each user account in the corpus. It is possible to identify the county associated with the latitude and longitude, and then to obtain county-level demographic statistics from the United States census. An **approximate** average demographic profile for each word in the study can be constructed by aggregating the demographic statistics for the counties of residence of each author who has used the word. Twitter users do not comprise an unbiased sample from each county, so this profile can only describe the demographic environment of the authors, and not the demographic properties of the authors themselves.

Results are shown in Figure 1. The confidence intervals reflect the Bonferroni correction for multiple comparison, setting $\alpha = 0.05/48$. The con-

[2](Stepwise) logistic regression has a long history in variationist sociolinguistics, particularly through the ubiquitous VARBRUL software (Tagliamonte, 2006).

[3]An L2 regularization parameter was selected by randomly sampling 50 training/test splits. Average accuracy was between 58% and 66% on the development data, for the optimal regularization coefficient.

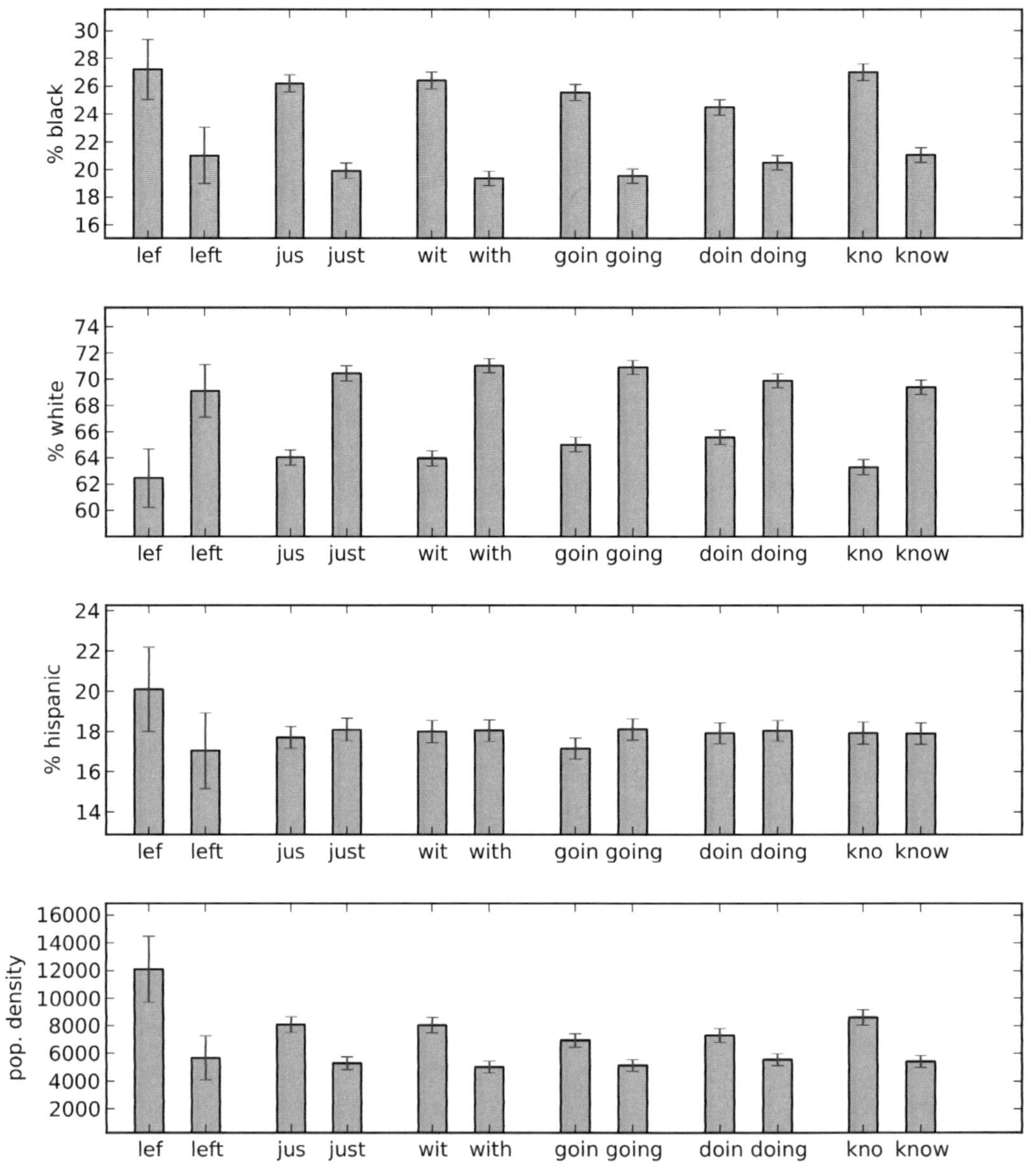


Figure 1: Average demographics of the counties in which users of each term live, with 95% confidence intervals

sonant cluster reduction examples are indeed preferred by authors from densely-populated (urban) counties with more African Americans, although these counties tend to prefer *all* of the non-standard variants, including the control pair *kno/know*. Conversely, the non-standard variants have aggregate demographic profiles that include fewer European Americans. None of the differences regarding the percentage of Hispanics/Latinos are statistically significant. Overall, these results show an association between non-standard orthography and densely-populated counties with high proportions of African Americans, but we find no special affinity for consonant cluster reduction.

## 7 Related work

Previous studies of the impact of dialect on writing have found relatively little evidence of purely phonological variation in written language. Whiteman (1982) gathered an oral/written dataset of interview transcripts and classroom compositions. In the written data, there are many examples of final consonant deletion: verbal *-s* (*he go- to the pool*), plural *-s* (*in their hand-*), possessive *-s* (*it is Sally- radio*), and past tense *-ed*. However, each of these deletions is morphosyntactic rather than purely phonological. They are seen by Whiteman as an omission of the inflectional suffix, rather than as a transcription of phonological variation, which she finds to be very rare in cases where morphosyntactic factors are not in play. She writes, "nonstandard phonological features rarely occur in writing, even when these features are extremely frequent in the oral dialect of the writer."

Similar evidence is presented by Thompson et al. (2004), who compare the spoken and written language of 50 third-grade students who were identified as speakers of African American English (AAE). While each of these students produced a substantial amount of AAE in spoken language, they produced only one third as many AAE features in the written sample. Thompson *et al.* find almost no instances of purely phonological features in writing, including consonant cluster reduction — except in combination with morphosyntactic features, such as zero past tense (e.g. *mother kiss(ed) them all goodbye*). They propose the following explanation:

> African American students have models for *spoken* AAE; however, children do not have models for written AAE... students likely have minimal opportunities to experience AAE in print (emphasis in the original).

This was written in 2004; in the intervening years, social media and text messages now provide many examples of written AAE. Unlike classroom settings, social media is informal and outside the scope of school control. Whether the increasing prevalence of written AAE will ultimately lead to widely-accepted writing systems for this and other dialects is an intriguing open question.

## 8 Conclusions and future work

The experiments in this paper demonstrate that phonology impacts social media orthography at the word level and beyond. I have discussed examples of three such phenomena: consonant cluster reduction, th-stopping, and the replacement of the velar nasal with the coronal ("g-dropping"). Both consonant cluster reduction and th-stopping are significantly influenced by the phonological context: their frequency depends on whether the subsequent segment begins with a vowel. This indicates that when social media authors transcribe spoken language variation, they are not simply replacing standard spellings of individual words. The more difficult question — *how* phonological context enters into writing — must be left for future work.

There are several other avenues along which to continue this research. The sociolinguistic literature describes a number of other systematic factors that impact consonant cluster reduction (Guy, 1991; Tagliamonte and Temple, 2005), and a complete model that included all such factors might shed additional light on this phenomenon. In such work it is typical to distinguish between different types of consonants; for example, Tagliamonte and Temple (2005) distinguish obstruents, glides, pauses, and the liquids /r/ and /l/. In addition, while this paper has equated consonant *letters* with consonant *sounds*, a more careful analysis might attempt to induce (or annotate) the pronunciation of the relevant words. The speech synthesis literature offers numerous such methods (Bisani and Ney, 2008), though social media text may pose new challenges, particularly for approaches that are based on generalizing from standard pronunciation dictionaries.

One might also ask whether the phonological system impacts all authors to the same extent. Labov (2007) distinguishes two forms of language change: *transmission*, where successive generations of children advance a sound change, and *diffusion*, where language contact leads adults to "borrow" aspects of other languages or dialects. Labov marshalls evidence from regional sound changes to show that transmission is generally more structural and regular, while diffusion is more superficial and irregular; this may be attributed to the ability of child language learners to recognize structural linguistic patterns. Does phonological context impact transcription equally among all authors in our data, or can we identify authors whose use of phonological transcription is particularly sensitive to context?

## Acknowledgments

Thanks to Brendan O'Connor for building the Twitter dataset that made this research possible. Thanks to the reviewers for their helpful comments.

## References

Jannis Androutsopoulos. 2011. Language change and digital media: a review of conceptions and evidence. In Nikolas Coupland and Tore Kristiansen, editors, *Standard Languages and Language Standards in a Changing Europe*. Novus, Oslo.

S. Argamon, M. Koppel, J. Pennebaker, and J. Schler. 2007. Mining the blogosphere: age, gender, and the varieties of self-expression. *First Monday*, 12(9).

Robert Bayley. 1994. Consonant cluster reduction in tejano english. *Language Variation and Change*, 6(03):303–326.

Maximilian Bisani and Hermann Ney. 2008. Joint-sequence models for grapheme-to-phoneme conversion. *Speech Commun.*, 50(5):434–451, May.

Marie-Hélène Côté. 2004. Consonant cluster simplification in Québec French. *Probus: International journal of Latin and Romance linguistics*, 16:151–201.

E. Dresner and S.C. Herring. 2010. Functions of the nonverbal in cmc: Emoticons and illocutionary force. *Communication Theory*, 20(3):249–268.

Jacob Eisenstein, Brendan O'Connor, Noah A. Smith, and Eric P. Xing. 2010. A latent variable model for geographic lexical variation. In *Proceedings of EMNLP*.

Jacob Eisenstein, Noah A. Smith, and Eric P. Xing. 2011. Discovering sociolinguistic associations with structured sparsity. In *Proceedings of ACL*.

Jacob Eisenstein, Brendan O'Connor, Noah A. Smith, and Eric P. Xing. 2012. Mapping the geographical diffusion of new words, October.

Jennifer Foster, Ozlem Cetinoglu, Joachim Wagner, Joseph Le Roux, Joakim Nivre, Deirdre Hogan, and Josef van Genabith. 2011. From news to comment: Resources and benchmarks for parsing the language of web 2.0. In *Proceedings of IJCNLP*.

Kevin Gimpel, Nathan Schneider, Brendan O'Connor, Dipanjan Das, Daniel Mills, Jacob Eisenstein, Michael Heilman, Dani Yogatama, Jeffrey Flanigan, and Noah A. Smith. 2011. Part-of-speech tagging for twitter: annotation, features, and experiments. In *Proceedings of ACL*.

Matthew J. Gordon, 2004. *A Handbook of Varieties of English*, chapter New York, Philadelphia, and other northern cities, pages 282–299. Volume 1 of Kortmann et al. (Kortmann et al., 2004).

Stephan Gouws, Dirk Hovy, and Donald Metzler. 2011. Unsupervised mining of lexical variants from noisy text. In *Proceedings of the First workshop on Unsupervised Learning in NLP*, pages 82–90, Edinburgh, Scotland, July. Association for Computational Linguistics.

Lisa J. Green. 2002. *African American English: A Linguistic Introduction*. Cambridge University Press, September.

Gregory R. Guy. 1991. Contextual conditioning in variable lexical phonology. *Language Variation and Change*, 3:223–239, June.

Bernd Kortmann, Edgar W. Schneider, and Kate Burridge et al., editors. 2004. *A Handbook of Varieties of English*, volume 1. Mouton de Gruyter, Berlin, Boston.

William Labov, Paul Cohen, Clarence Robins, and John Lewis. 1968. A study of the Non-Standard english of negro and puerto rican speakers in new york city. Technical report, United States Office of Education, Washington, DC.

William Labov. 2007. Transmission and diffusion. *Language*, 83(2):344–387.

Fred Morstatter, Jurgen Pfeffer, Huan Liu, and Kathleen M. Carley. 2013. Is the sample good enough? comparing data from twitter's streaming api with twitter's firehose. In *Proceedings of ICWSM*.

John C. Paolillo. 1996. Language choice on soc.culture.punjab. *Electronic Journal of Communication/La Revue Electronique de Communication*, 6(3).

Delip Rao, David Yarowsky, Abhishek Shreevats, and Manaswi Gupta. 2010. Classifying latent user attributes in twitter. In *Proceedings of Workshop on Search and mining user-generated contents*.

Alan Ritter, Sam Clark, Mausam, and Oren Etzioni. 2011. Named entity recognition in tweets: an experimental study. In *Proceedings of EMNLP*.

Otto Santa Ana. 1991. *Phonetic simplification processes in the English of the barrio: A cross-generational sociolinguistic study of the Chicanos of Los Angeles*. Ph.D. thesis, University of Pennsylvania.

Aaron Smith and Joanna Brewer. 2012. Twitter use 2012. Technical report, Pew Research Center, May.

Sali Tagliamonte and Rosalind Temple. 2005. New perspectives on an ol' variable: (t,d) in british english. *Language Variation and Change*, 17:281–302, September.

Sali A. Tagliamonte. 2006. *Analysing Sociolinguistic Variation*. Cambridge University Press.

Erik R Thomas, 2004. *A Handbook of Varieties of English*, chapter Rural Southern white accents, pages 87–114. Volume 1 of Kortmann et al. (Kortmann et al., 2004).

Connie A. Thompson, Holly K. Craig, and Julie A. Washington. 2004. Variable production of african american english across oracy and literacy contexts. *Language, speech, and hearing services in schools*, 35(3):269–282, July.

Jeffrey S. Vitter. 1985. Random sampling with a reservoir. *ACM Trans. Math. Softw.*, 11(1):37–57, March.

Larry Wasserman. 2005. *All of Nonparametric Statistics (Springer Texts in Statistics)*. Springer, October.

Marcia F. Whiteman. 1982. Dialect influence in writing. In Marcia Farr Whiteman and Carl, editors, *Writing: The Nature, Development, and Teaching of Written Communication*, volume 1: Variation in writing. Routledge, October.

Benjamin Wing and Jason Baldridge. 2011. Simple supervised document geolocation with geodesic grids. In *Proceedings of ACL*.

# A Preliminary Study of Tweet Summarization using Information Extraction

**Wei Xu, Ralph Grishman, Adam Meyers**
Computer Science Department
New York University
New York, NY 10003, USA
{xuwei,grishman,meyers}@cs.nyu.edu

**Alan Ritter**
Computer Science and Engineering
University of Washington
Seattle, WA 98125, USA
aritter@cs.washington.edu

## Abstract

Although the ideal length of summaries differs greatly from topic to topic on Twitter, previous work has only generated summaries of a pre-fixed length. In this paper, we propose an event-graph based method using information extraction techniques that is able to create summaries of variable length for different topics. In particular, we extend the Pagerank-like ranking algorithm from previous work to partition event graphs and thereby detect fine-grained aspects of the event to be summarized. Our preliminary results show that summaries created by our method are more concise and news-worthy than SumBasic according to human judges. We also provide a brief survey of datasets and evaluation design used in previous work to highlight the need of developing a standard evaluation for automatic tweet summarization task.

## 1 Introduction

Tweets contain a wide variety of useful information from many perspectives about important events taking place in the world. The huge number of messages, many containing irrelevant and redundant information, quickly leads to a situation of information overload. This motivates the need for automatic summarization systems which can select a few messages for presentation to a user which cover the most important information relating to the event without redundancy and filter out irrelevant and personal information that is not of interest beyond the user's immediate social network.

Although there is much recent work focusing on the task of multi-tweet summarization (Becker et al., 2011; Inouye and Kalita, 2011; Zubiaga et al., 2012; Liu et al., 2011a; Takamura et al., 2011; Harabagiu and Hickl, 2011; Wei et al., 2012), most previous work relies only on surface lexical clues, redundancy and social network specific signals (e.g. user relationship), and little work has considered taking limited advantage of information extraction techniques (Harabagiu and Hickl, 2011) in generative models. Because of the noise and redundancy in social media posts, the performance of off-the-shelf news-trained natural language process systems is degraded while simple term frequency is proven powerful for summarizing tweets (Inouye and Kalita, 2011). A natural and interesting research question is whether it is beneficial to extract named entities and events in the tweets as has been shown for classic multi-document summarization (Li et al., 2006). Recent progress on building NLP tools for Twitter (Ritter et al., 2011; Gimpel et al., 2011; Liu et al., 2011b; Ritter et al., 2012; Liu et al., 2012) makes it possible to investigate an approach to summarizing Twitter events which is based on Information Extraction techniques.

We investigate a graph-based approach which leverages named entities, event phrases and their connections across tweets. A similar idea has been studied by Li et al. (2006) to rank the salience of event concepts in summarizing news articles. However, the extreme redundancy and simplicity of tweets allows us to explicitly split the event graph into subcomponents that cover various aspects of the initial event to be summarized to create comprehen-

| Work | Dataset (size of each cluster) | System Output | Evaluation Metrics |
|---|---|---|---|
| Inouye and Kalita (2011) | trending topics (approximately 1500 tweets) | 4 tweets | ROUGE and human (overall quality comparing to human summary) |
| Sharifi et al. (2010) | same as above | 1 tweet | same as above |
| Rosa et al. (2011) | segmented hashtag topics by LDA and k-means clustering (average 410 tweets) | 1, 5, 10 tweets | Precision@k (relevance to topic) |
| Harabagiu and Hickl (2011) | real-word event topics (a minimum of 2500 tweets) | top tweets until a limit of 250 words was reached | human (coverage and coherence) |
| Liu et al. (2011a) | general topics and hashtag topics (average 1.7k tweets) | same lengths as of the human summary, vary for each topic (about 2 or 3 tweets) | ROUGE and human (content coverage, grammaticality, non-redundancy, referential clarity, focus) |
| Wei et al. (2012) | segmented hashtag topics according to burstiness (average 10k tweets) | 10 tweets | ROUGE, Precison/Recall (good readability and rich content) |
| Takamura et al. (2011) | specific soccer games (2.8k - 5.2k tweets) | same lengths as the human summary, vary for each topic (26 - 41 tweets) | ROUGE (considering only content words) |
| Chakrabarti and Punera (2011) | specific football games (1.8k tweets) | 10 - 70 tweets | Precision@k (relevance to topic) |

Table 1: Summary of datasets and evaluation metrics used in several previous work on tweet summarization

sive and non-redundant summaries. Our work is the first to use a Pagerank-like algorithm for graph partitioning and ranking in the context of summarization, and the first to generate tweet summaries of variable length which is particularly important for tweet summarization. Unlike news articles, the amount of information in a set of topically clustered tweets varies greatly, from very repetitive to very discrete. For example, the tweets about one album release can be more or less paraphrases, while those about another album by a popular singer may involve rumors and release events etc. In the human study conducted by Inouye and Kalita (2011), annotators strongly prefer different numbers of tweets in a summary for different topics. However, most of the previous work produced summaries of a pre-fixed length and has no evaluation on conciseness. Liu et al. (2011a) and Takamura et al. (2011) also noticed the ideal length of summaries can be very different from topic to topic, and had to use the length of human reference summaries to decide the length of system outputs, information which is not available in practice. In contrast, we developed a system that is capable of detecting fine-grained sub-events and generating summaries with the proper number of representative tweets accordingly for different topics.

Our experimental results show that with information extraction it is possible to create more meaningful and concise summaries. Tweets that contain real-world events are usually more informative and readable. Event-based summarization is especially beneficial in this situation due to the fact that tweets are short and self-contained with simple discourse structure. The boundary of 140 characters makes it efficient to extract semi-structured events with shallow natural language processing techniques and re-

| Tweets (Date Created) | Named Entity | Event Phrases | Date Mentioned |
|---|---|---|---|
| Nooooo.. Season premiere of Doctor Who is on Sept 1 world wide and we'll be at World Con (8/22/2012) | doctor who, world con | season, is on, premiere | sept 1 (9/1/2012) |
| guess what I DON'T get to do tomorrow! WATCH DOCTOR WHO (8/31/2012) | doctor who | watch | tomorrow (9/1/2012) |
| As I missed it on Saturday, I'm now catching up on Doctor Who (9/4/2012) | doctor who | missed, catching up | saturday (9/1/2012) |
| Rumour: Nokia could announce two WP8 devices on September 5 http://t.co/yZUwDFLV (via @mobigyaan) | nokia, wp8 | announce | september 5 (9/5/2012) |
| Verizon and Motorola won't let Nokia have all the fun ; scheduling September 5th in New York http://t.co/qbBlYnSl (8/19/2012) | nokia, verizon, motorola, new york | scheduling | september 5th (9/5/2012) |
| Don't know if it's excitement or rooting for the underdog, but I am genuinely excited for Nokia come Sept 5: http://t.co/UhV5SUMP (8/7/2012) | nokia | rooting, excited | sept 5 (9/5/2012) |

Table 2: Event-related information extracted from tweets

duces the complexity of the relationship (or no relationship) between events according to their co-occurrence, resulting in differences in constructing event graphs from previous work in news domain (Li et al., 2006).

## 2 Issues in Current Research on Tweet Summarization

The most serious problem in tweet summarization is that there is no standard dataset, and consequently no standard evaluation methodology. Although there are more than a dozen recent works on social media summarization, astonishingly, almost each research group used a different dataset and a different experiment setup. This is largely attributed to the difficulty of defining the right granularity of a topic in Twitter. In Table 1, we summarize the experiment designs of several selective works. Regardless of the differences, researchers generally agreed on :

- clustering tweets topically and temporally
- generating either a very short summary for a focused topic or a long summary for large-size clusters
- difficulty and necessity to generate summaries of variable length for different topics

Although the need of variable-length summaries have been raised in previous work, none has provide a good solution (Liu et al., 2011a; Takamura et al., 2011; Inouye and Kalita, 2011). In this paper, our focus is study the feasibility of generating concise summaries of variable length and improving meaningfulness by using information extraction techniques. We hope this study can provide new insights on the task and help in developing a standard evaluation in the future.

## 3 Approach

We first extract event information including named entities and event phrases from tweets and construct event graphs that represent the relationship between them. We then rank and partition the events using PageRank-like algorithms, and create summaries of variable length for different topics.

### 3.1 Event Extraction from Tweets

As a first step towards summarizing popular events discussed on Twitter, we need a way to identify events from Tweets. We utilize several natural language processing tools that specially developed for noisy text to extract text phrases that bear essential event information, including named entities (Ritter et al., 2011), event-referring phrases (Ritter et al.,

2012) and temporal expressions (Mani and Wilson, 2000). Both the named entity and event taggers utilize Conditional Random Fields models (Lafferty, 2001) trained on annotated data, while the temporal expression resolver uses a mix of hand-crafted and machine-learned rules. Example event information extracted from Tweets are presented in Table 2.

The self-contained nature of tweets allows efficient extraction of event information without deep analysis (e.g. co-reference resolution). On the other hand, individual tweets are also very terse, often lacking sufficient context to access the importance of events. It is crucial to exploit the highly redundancy in Twitter. Closely following previous work by Ritter et al. (2012), we group together sets of topically and temporally related tweets, which mention the same named entity and a temporal reference resolved to the same unique calendar date. We also employ a statistical significance test to measure strength of association between each named entity and date, and thereby identify important events discussed widely among users with a specific focus, such as the release of a new iPhone as opposed to individual users discussing everyday events involving their phones. By discarding frequent but insignificant events, we can produce more meaningful summaries about popular real-world events.

### 3.2 Event Graphs

Since tweets have simple discourse and are self-contained, it is a reasonable assumption that named entities and event phrases that co-occurred together in a single tweet are very likely related. Given a collection of tweets, we represent such connections by a weighted undirected graph :

- Nodes: named entities and event phrases are represented by nodes and treated indifferently.
- Edges: two nodes are connected by an undirected edge if they co-occurred in $k$ tweets, and the weight of edge is $k$.

We find it helpful to merge named entities and event phrases that have lexical overlap if they are frequent but not the topic of the tweet cluster. For example, 'bbc', 'radio 1', 'bbc radio 1' are combined together in a set of tweets about a band. Figure 1 shows a very small toy example of event graph. In the experiments of this paper, we also exclude the edges with $k < 2$ to reduce noise in the data and calculation cost.

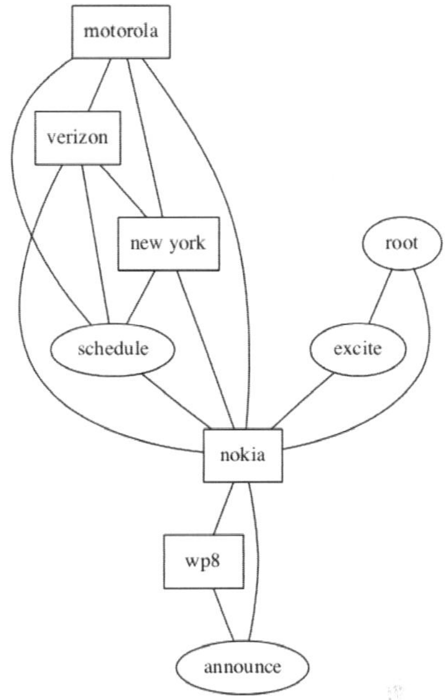


Figure 1: A toy event graph example built from the three sentences of the event 'Nokia - 9/5/2012' in Table 2

### 3.3 Event Ranking and Partitioning

Graph-based ranking algorithms are widely used in automatic summarization to decide salience of concepts or sentences based on global information recursively drawn from the entire graph. We adapt the PageRank-like algorithm used in TextRank (Mihalcea and Tarau, 2004) that takes into account edge weights when computing the score associated with a vertex in the graph.

Formally, let $G = (V, E)$ be a undirected graph with the set of vertices $V$ and set of edges $E$, where $E$ is a subset of $V \times V$. For a given vertex $V_i$, let $Ad(V_i)$ be the set of vertices that adjacent to it. The weight of the edge between $V_i$ and $V_j$ is denoted as $w_{ij}$, and $w_{ij} = w_{ji}$. The score of a vertex $V_i$ is defined as follows:

$$S(V_i) = (1-d) + d \times \sum_{V_j \in Ad(V_i)} \frac{w_{ij} \times S(V_j)}{\sum_{V_k \in Ad(V_j)} w_{jk}}$$

where $d$ is a damping factor that is usually set to 0.85 (Brin and Page, 1998), and this is the value we are also using in our implementation.

Starting from arbitrary values assigned to each node in the graph, the computation iterates until convergence. Note that the final salience score of each node is not affected by the choice of the initial values assigned to each node in the graph, but rather the weights of edges.

In previous work computed scores are then used directly to select text fractions for summaries (Li et al., 2006). However, the redundancy and simplicity of tweets allow further exploration into sub-event detection by graph partitioning. The intuition is that the correlations between named entities and event phrases within same sub-events are much stronger than between sub-events. This phenomena is more obvious and clear in tweet than in news articles, where events are more diverse and complicated related to each other given lengthy context.

As theoretically studied in local partitioning problem (Andersen et al., 2006), a good partition of the graph can be obtained by separating high ranked vertices from low ranked vertices, if the nodes in the graph have ranks that are distinguishable. Utilizing a similar idea, we show that a simple greedy algorithm is efficient to find important sub-events and generate useful summaries in our tasks. As shown in Figure 2 and 3, the high ranked nodes (whose scores are greater than 1, the average score of all nodes in the graph) in tweet event graphs show the divisions within a topic. We search for strongly connected sub-graphs, as gauged by parameter $\alpha$, from the highest ranked node to lower ranked ones.The proportion of tweets in a set that are related to a sub-event is then estimated according to the ratio between the sum of node scores in the sub-graph versus the entire graph. We select one tweet for each sub-event that best covers the related nodes with the highest sum of node scores normalized by length as summaries. By adding a cutoff (parameter $\beta$) on proportion of sub-event required to be included into summaries, we can produce summaries with the appropriate length according to the diversity of information in a set of tweets.

In Figure 2, 3 and 4, the named entity which is also the topic of tweet cluster is omitted since it is connected with every node in the event graph. The size of node represents the salience score, while the shorter, straighter and more vertical the edge is, the higher its weight. The nodes with rectangle shapes are named entities, while round shaped ones are event phrases. Note that in most cases, sub-events correspond to connected components in the event graph of high ranked nodes as in Figure 2 and 3. However, our simple greedy algorithm also allows multiple sub-events for a single connected component that can not be covered by one tweet in the summary. For example, in Figure 4, two sub-events $e_1 = \{sell, delete, start, payment\}$ and $e_2 = \{facebook, share\ user\ data, privacy\ policy, debut\}$ are chosen to accommodate the complex event.

**Algorithm 1** Find important sub-events

**Require:** Ranked event graph $G = (V, E)$, the named entity $V_0$ which is the topic of event cluster, parameters $\alpha$ and $\beta$ that can be set towards user preference over development data

Initialize the pool of high ranked nodes $\tilde{V} \leftarrow \{V_i | \forall V_i \in V, S(V_i) > 1\} - V_0$ and the total weight $W \leftarrow \sum_{V_i \in \tilde{V}} S(V_i)$<br>
**while** $\tilde{V} \neq \emptyset$ **do**<br>
  Pop the highest ranked node $V_m$ from $\tilde{V}$<br>
  Put $V_m$ to a temporary sub-event $e \leftarrow \{V_m\}$<br>
  **for all** $V_n$ in $\tilde{V}$ **do**<br>
    **if** $w_{mn}/w_{0m} > \alpha$ and $w_{0n}/w_{0m} > \alpha$ **then**<br>
      $e \leftarrow e \cup \{V_n\}$<br>
    **end if**<br>
  **end for**<br>
  $W_e \leftarrow \sum_{V_i \in e} S(V_i)$<br>
  **if** $W_e/W > \beta$ **then**<br>
    Successfully find a sub-event $e$<br>
    Remove all nodes in $e$ from $\tilde{V}$<br>
  **end if**<br>
**end while**

## 4 Experiments

### 4.1 Data

We gathered tweets over a 4-month period spanning November 2012 to February 2013 using the Twitter Streaming API. As described in more details in previous work on Twitter event extraction by Ritter et al. (2012), we grouped together all tweets which mention the same named entity (recognized using

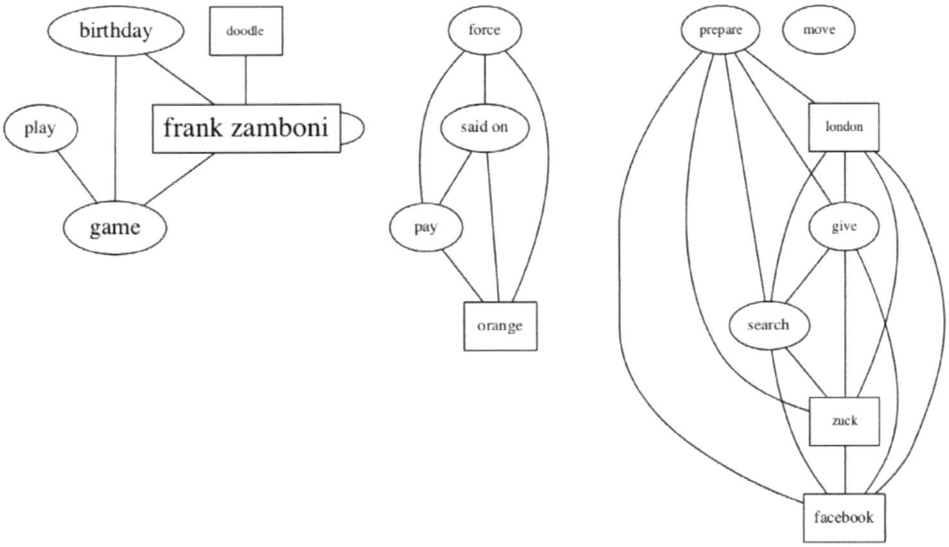


Figure 2: Event graph of 'Google - 1/16/2013', an example of event cluster with multiple focuses

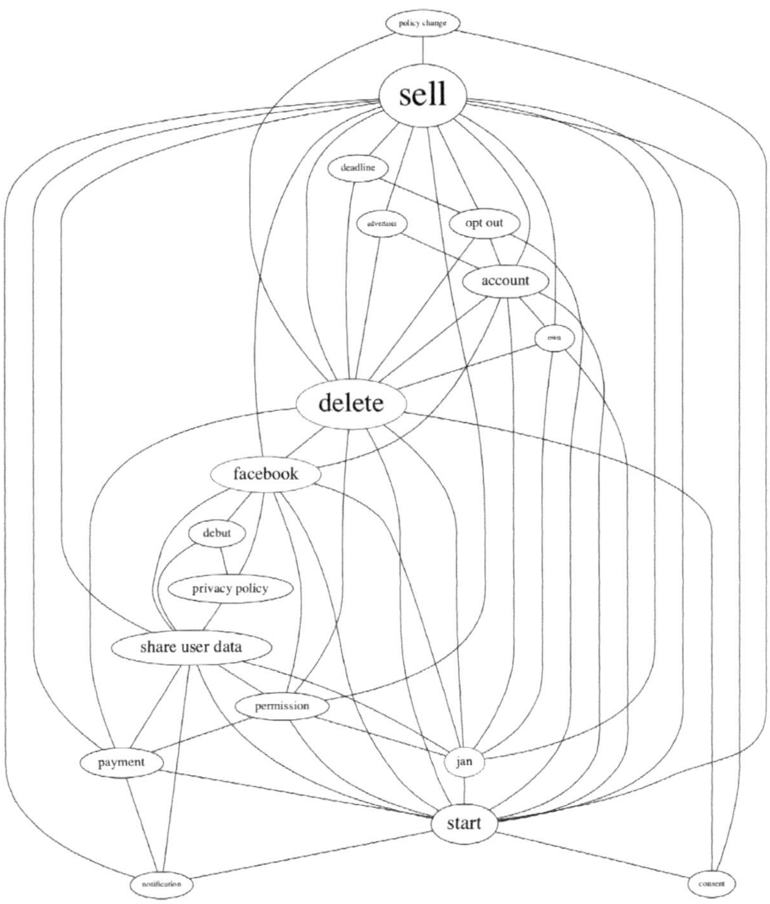


Figure 3: Event graph of 'Instagram - 1/16/2013', an example of event cluster with a single but complex focus

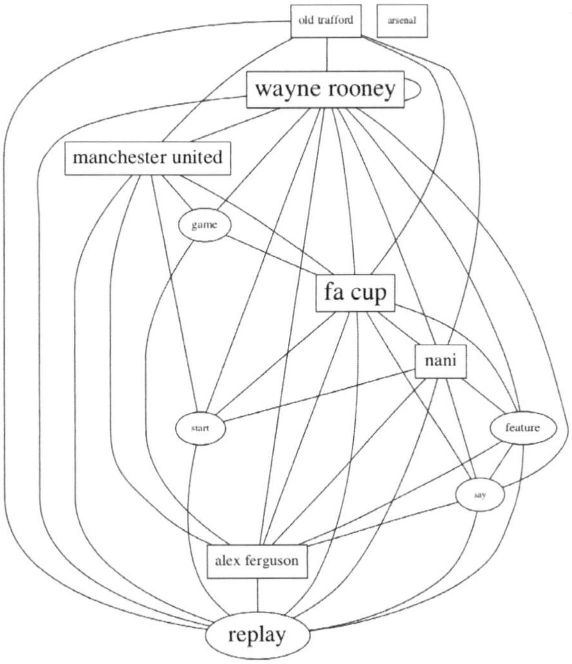


Figure 4: Event graph of 'West Ham - 1/16/2013', an example of event cluster with a single focus

a Twitter specific name entity tagger[1]) and a reference to the same unique calendar date (resolved using a temporal expression processor (Mani and Wilson, 2000)). Tweets published during the whole period are aggregated together to find top events that happen on each calendar day. We applied the $G^2$ test for statistical significance (Dunning, 1993) to rank the event clusters, considering the corpus frequency of the named entity, the number of times the date has been mentioned, and the number of tweets which mention both together. We randomly picked the events of one day for human evaluation, that is the day of January 16, 2013 with 38 events and an average of 465 tweets per event cluster.

For each cluster, our systems produce two versions of summaries, one with a fixed number (set to 3) of tweets and another one with a flexible number (vary from 1 to 4) of tweets. Both $\alpha$ and $\beta$ are set to 0.1 in our implementation. All parameters are set experimentally over a small development dataset consisting of 10 events in Twitter data of September 2012.

### 4.2 Baseline

SumBasic (Vanderwende et al., 2007) is a simple and effective summarization approach based on term frequency, which we use as our baseline. It uses word probabilities with an update function to avoid redundancy to select sentences or posts in a social media setting. It is shown to outperform three other well-known multi-document summarization methods, namely LexRank (Erkan and Radev, 2004), TextRank (Mihalcea and Tarau, 2004) and MEAD (Radev et al., 2004) on tweets in (Inouye and Kalita, 2011), possibly because that the relationship between tweets is much simpler than between sentences in news articles and can be well captured by simple frequency methods. The improvement over the LexRank model on tweets is gained by considering the number of retweets and influential users is another side-proof (Wei et al., 2012) of the effectiveness of frequency.

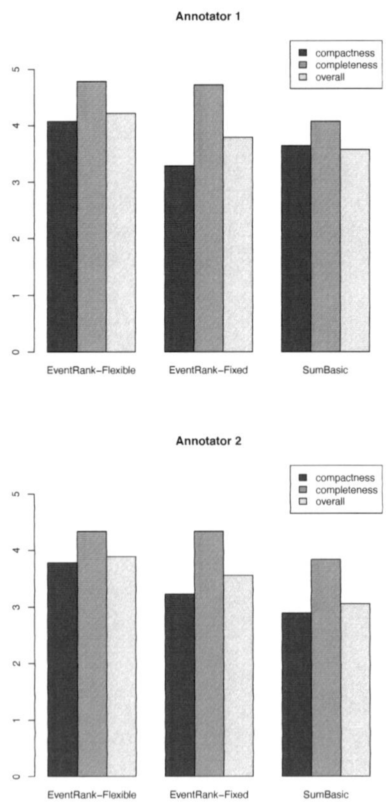


Figure 5: human judgments evaluating tweet summarization systems

[1] https://github.com/aritter/twitter_nlp

| Event | System | Summary |
|---|---|---|
| Google 1/16/2013 | EventRank (Flexible) | - Google 's home page is a Zamboni game in celebration of Frank Zamboni 's birthday January 16 #GameOn<br>- Today social , Tomorrow Google ! Facebook Has Publicly Redefined Itself As A Search Company http://t.co/dAevB2V0 via @sai<br>- Orange says has it has forced Google to pay for traffic . The Head of the Orange said on Wednesday it had ... http://t.co/dOqAHhWi |
| | SumBasic | - Tomorrow's Google doodle is going to be a Zamboni! I may have to take a vacation day.<br>- the game on google today reminds me of hockey #tooexcited #saturday<br>- The fact that I was soooo involved in that google doodle game says something about this Wednesday #TGIW You should try it! |
| Instagram 1/16/2013 | EventRank (Flexible) | - So Instagram can sell your pictures to advertisers without u knowing starting January 16th I'm bout to delete my instagram !<br>- Instagram debuts new privacy policy , set to share user data with Facebook beginning January 16 |
| | SumBasic | - Instagram will have the rights to sell your photos to Advertisers as of jan 16<br>- Over for Instagram on January 16th<br>- Instagram says it now has the right to sell your photos unless you delete your account by January 16th http://t.co/tsjic6yA |
| West Ham 1/16/2013 | EventRank (Flexible) | - RT @Bassa_Mufc : Wayne Rooney and Nani will feature in the FA Cup replay with West Ham on Wednesday - Sir Alex Ferguson |
| | SumBasic | - Wayne Rooney could be back to face West Ham in next Wednesday's FA Cup replay at Old Trafford. #BPL<br>- Tomorrow night come on West Ham lol<br>- Nani's fit abd WILL play tomorrow against West Ham! Sir Alex confirmed :) |

Table 3: Event-related information extracted from tweets

### 4.3 Preliminary Results

We performed a human evaluation in which two annotators were asked to rate the system on a five-point scale (1=very poor, 5=very good) for completeness and compactness. Completeness refers to how well the summary cover the important content in the tweets. Compactness refers to how much meaningful and non-redundant information is in the summary. Because the tweets were collected according to information extraction results and ranked by salience, the readability of summaries generated by different systems are generally very good. The top 38 events of January 16, 2013 are used as test set. The aggregate results of the human evaluation are displayed in Figure 5. Agreement between annotators measured using Pearson's Correlation Coefficient is 0.59, 0.62, 0.62 respectively for compactness, completeness and overall judgements.

Results suggest that the models described in this paper produce more satisfactory results as the baseline approaches. The improvement of EventRank-Flexible over SumBasic is significant (two-tailed $p < 0.05$) for all three metrics according to student's $t$ test. Example summaries of the events in Figure 2, 3 and 4 are presented respectively in Table 3. The advantages of our method are the following: 1) it finds important facts of real-world events 2) it prefers tweets with good readability 3) it includes the right amount of information with diversity and without redundancy. For example, our system picked only one tweet about 'West Ham -1/16/2013' that convey the same message as the three tweets together of the baseline system. For another example, among the tweets about Google around 1/16/2013, users intensively talk about the Google doodle game with a very wide range of words creatively, giving word-based methods a hard time to pick up the diverse and essential event information that is less frequent.

## 5 Conclusions and Future Work

We present an initial study of feasibility to generate compact summaries of variable lengths for tweet summarization by extending a Pagerank-like algorithm to partition event graphs. The evaluation shows that information extraction techniques are helpful to generate news-worthy summaries of good readability from tweets.

In the future, we are interested in improving the approach and evaluation, studying automatic metrics to evaluate summarization of variable length and getting involved in developing a standard evaluation for tweet summarization tasks. We wonder whether other graph partitioning algorithms may improve the performance. We also consider extending this graph-based approach to disambiguate named entities or resolve event coreference in Twitter data. Another direction of future work is to extend the proposed approach to different data, for example, temporal-aware clustered tweets etc.

## Acknowledgments

This research was supported in part by NSF grant IIS-0803481, ONR grant N00014-08-1-0431, and DARPA contract FA8750- 09-C-0179, and carried out at the University of Washington's Turing Center.

We thank Mausam and Oren Etzioni of University of Washington, Maria Pershina of New York University for their advice.

## References

Reid Andersen, Fan Chung, and Kevin Lang. 2006. Local graph partitioning using pagerank vectors. In *Foundations of Computer Science, 2006. FOCS'06. 47th Annual IEEE Symposium on*, pages 475–486. IEEE.

Hila Becker, Mor Naaman, and Luis Gravano. 2011. Selecting quality twitter content for events. In *Proceedings of the Fifth International AAAI Conference on Weblogs and Social Media (ICWSM'11)*.

Sergey Brin and Lawrence Page. 1998. The anatomy of a large-scale hypertextual web search engine. *Computer networks and ISDN systems*, 30(1):107–117.

Deepayan Chakrabarti and Kunal Punera. 2011. Event summarization using tweets. In *Proceedings of the Fifth International AAAI Conference on Weblogs and Social Media*, pages 66–73.

Ted Dunning. 1993. Accurate methods for the statistics of surprise and coincidence. *Computational linguistics*, 19(1):61–74.

Günes Erkan and Dragomir R. Radev. 2004. Lexrank: Graph-based lexical centrality as salience in text summarization. *J. Artif. Intell. Res. (JAIR)*, 22:457–479.

Kevin Gimpel, Nathan Schneider, Brendan O'Connor, Dipanjan Das, Daniel Mills, Jacob Eisenstein, Michael Heilman, Dani Yogatama, Jeffrey Flanigan, and Noah A. Smith. 2011. Part-of-speech tagging for twitter: Annotation, features, and experiments. In *ACL*.

Sanda Harabagiu and Andrew Hickl. 2011. Relevance modeling for microblog summarization. In *Fifth International AAAI Conference on Weblogs and Social Media*.

David Inouye and Jugal K Kalita. 2011. Comparing twitter summarization algorithms for multiple post summaries. In *Privacy, security, risk and trust (passat), 2011 ieee third international conference on and 2011 ieee third international conference on social computing (socialcom)*, pages 298–306. IEEE.

John Lafferty. 2001. Conditional random fields: Probabilistic models for segmenting and labeling sequence data. pages 282–289. Morgan Kaufmann.

Wenjie Li, Wei Xu, Chunfa Yuan, Mingli Wu, and Qin Lu. 2006. Extractive summarization using inter- and intra- event relevance. In *Proceedings of the 21st International Conference on Computational Linguistics and the 44th annual meeting of the Association for Computational Linguistics*, ACL-44, pages 369–376, Stroudsburg, PA, USA. Association for Computational Linguistics.

Fei Liu, Yang Liu, and Fuliang Weng. 2011a. Why is ÒsxswÓ trending? exploring multiple text sources for twitter topic summarization. *ACL HLT 2011*, page 66.

Xiaohua Liu, Shaodian Zhang, Furu Wei, and Ming Zhou. 2011b. Recognizing named entities in tweets. In *ACL*.

Xiaohua Liu, Furu Wei, Ming Zhou, et al. 2012. Quickview: Nlp-based tweet search. In *Proceedings of the ACL 2012 System Demonstrations*, pages 13–18. Association for Computational Linguistics.

Inderjeet Mani and George Wilson. 2000. Robust temporal processing of news. In *Proceedings of the 38th An-*

*nual Meeting on Association for Computational Linguistics*, ACL '00, pages 69–76, Stroudsburg, PA, USA. Association for Computational Linguistics.

Rada Mihalcea and Paul Tarau. 2004. Textrank: Bringing order into texts. In *Proceedings of EMNLP*, volume 4, pages 404–411. Barcelona, Spain.

Dragomir Radev, Timothy Allison, Sasha Blair-Goldensohn, John Blitzer, Arda Celebi, Stanko Dimitrov, Elliott Drabek, Ali Hakim, Wai Lam, Danyu Liu, et al. 2004. Mead-a platform for multidocument multilingual text summarization. In *Proceedings of LREC*, volume 2004.

Alan Ritter, Sam Clark, Mausam, and Oren Etzioni. 2011. Named entity recognition in tweets: An experimental study.

Alan Ritter, Mausam, Oren Etzioni, and Sam Clark. 2012. Open domain event extraction from twitter. In *KDD*, pages 1104–1112. ACM.

Kevin Dela Rosa, Rushin Shah, Bo Lin, Anatole Gershman, and Robert Frederking. 2011. Topical clustering of tweets. *Proceedings of the ACM SIGIR: SWSM*.

Beaux Sharifi, Mark-Anthony Hutton, and Jugal K Kalita. 2010. Experiments in microblog summarization. In *Proc. of IEEE Second International Conference on Social Computing*.

Hiroya Takamura, Hikaru Yokono, and Manabu Okumura. 2011. Summarizing a document stream. *Advances in Information Retrieval*, pages 177–188.

Lucy Vanderwende, Hisami Suzuki, Chris Brockett, and Ani Nenkova. 2007. Beyond sumbasic: Task-focused summarization with sentence simplification and lexical expansion. *Information Processing & Management*, 43(6):1606–1618.

Furu Wei, Ming Zhou, and Heung-Yeung Shum. 2012. Twitter topic summarization by ranking tweets using social influence and content quality. In *COLING*.

Arkaitz Zubiaga, Damiano Spina, Enrique Amigó, and Julio Gonzalo. 2012. Towards real-time summarization of scheduled events from twitter streams. In *Proceedings of the 23rd ACM conference on Hypertext and social media*, pages 319–320. ACM.

# Really? Well. Apparently Bootstrapping Improves the Performance of Sarcasm and Nastiness Classifiers for Online Dialogue

**Stephanie Lukin**
Natural Language and Dialogue Systems
University of California, Santa Cruz
1156 High Street, Santa Cruz, CA 95064
slukin@soe.ucsc.edu

**Marilyn Walker**
Natural Language and Dialogue Systems
University of California, Santa Cruz
1156 High Street, Santa Cruz, CA 95064
maw@soe.ucsc.edu

## Abstract

More and more of the information on the web is dialogic, from Facebook newsfeeds, to forum conversations, to comment threads on news articles. In contrast to traditional, monologic Natural Language Processing resources such as news, highly social dialogue is frequent in social media, making it a challenging context for NLP. This paper tests a bootstrapping method, originally proposed in a monologic domain, to train classifiers to identify two different types of subjective language in dialogue: sarcasm and nastiness. We explore two methods of developing linguistic indicators to be used in a first level classifier aimed at maximizing precision at the expense of recall. The best performing classifier for the first phase achieves 54% precision and 38% recall for sarcastic utterances. We then use general syntactic patterns from previous work to create more general sarcasm indicators, improving precision to 62% and recall to 52%. To further test the generality of the method, we then apply it to bootstrapping a classifier for nastiness dialogic acts. Our first phase, using crowdsourced nasty indicators, achieves 58% precision and 49% recall, which increases to 75% precision and 62% recall when we bootstrap over the first level with generalized syntactic patterns.

## 1 Introduction

More and more of the information on the web is dialogic, from Facebook newsfeeds, to forum conversations, to comment threads on news articles. In contrast to traditional, monologic Natural Language Processing resources such as news, highly social dialogue is very frequent in social media, as illustrated in the snippets in Fig. 1 from the publicly available Internet Argument Corpus (**IAC**) (Walker et al., 2012). Utterances are frequently sarcastic, e.g., *Really? Well, when I have a kid, I'll be sure to just leave it in the woods, since it can apparently care for itself* (R2 in Fig. 1 as well as Q1 and R1), and are often nasty, e.g. *Here come the Christians, thinking they can know everything by guessing, and commiting the genetic fallacy left and right* (R3 in Fig. 1). Note also the frequent use of dialogue specific discourse cues, e.g. the use of *No* in R1, *Really? Well* in R2, and *okay, well* in Q3 in Fig. 1 (Fox Tree and Schrock, 1999; Bryant and Fox Tree, 2002; Fox Tree, 2010).

| Quote **Q**, Response **R** | **Sarc** | **Nasty** |
|---|---|---|
| **Q1**: I jsut voted. sorry if some people actually have, you know, LIVES and don't sit around all day on debate forums to cater to some atheists posts that he thiks they should drop everything for. emoticon-rolleyes emoticon-rolleyes emoticon-rolleyes As to the rest of your post, well, from your attitude I can tell you are not Christian in the least. Therefore I am content in knowing where people that spew garbage like this will end up in the End. | | |
| **R1**: No, let me guess . . . er . . . McDonalds. No, Disneyland. Am I getting closer? | 1 | -3.6 |
| **Q2**: The key issue is that once children are born they are not physically dependent on a particular individual. | | |
| **R2** Really? Well, when I have a kid, I'll be sure to just leave it in the woods, since it can apparently care for itself. | 1 | -1 |
| **Q3**: okay, well i think that you are just finding reasons to go against Him. I think that you had some bad experiances when you were younger or a while ago that made you turn on God. You are looking for reasons, not very good ones i might add, to convince people.....either way, God loves you. :) | | |
| **R3**: Here come the Christians, thinking they can know everything by guessing, and commiting the genetic fallacy left and right. | 0.8 | -3.4 |

Figure 1: Sample Quote/Response Pairs from 4forums.com with Mechanical Turk annotations for Sarcasm and Nasty/Nice. Highly negative values of Nasty/Nice indicate strong nastiness and sarcasm is indicated by values near 1.

The IAC comes with annotations of different types of social language categories including sarcastic vs not sarcastic, nasty vs nice, rational vs emotional and respectful vs insulting. Using a conservative threshold of agreement amongst the annotators, an analysis of 10,003 Quote/Response pairs (Q/R pairs) from the `4forums` portion of IAC suggests that social subjective language is fairly frequent: about 12% of posts are sarcastic, 23% are emotional, and 12% are insulting or nasty. We select sarcastic and nasty dialogic turns to test our method on more than one type of subjective language and explore issues of generalization; we do not claim any relationship between these types of social language in this work.

Despite their frequency, expanding this corpus of sarcastic or nasty utterances at scale is expensive: human annotation of 100% of the corpus would be needed to identify 12% more examples of sarcasm or nastiness. An explanation of how utterances are annotated in IAC is detailed in Sec. 2.

Our aim in this paper is to explore whether it is possible to extend a method for bootstrapping a classifier for monologic, subjective sentences proposed by Riloff & Wiebe, henceforth R&W (Riloff and Wiebe, 2003; Thelen and Riloff, 2002), to automatically find sarcastic and nasty utterances in unannotated online dialogues. Sec. 3 provides an overview of R&W's bootstrapping method. To apply bootstrapping, we:

1. Explore two different methods for identifying cue words and phrases in two types of subjective language in dialogues: sarcasm and nasty (Sec. 4);
2. Use the learned indicators to train a sarcastic (nasty) dialogue act classifier that maximizes precision at the expense of recall (Sec. 5);
3. Use the classified utterances to learn general syntactic extraction patterns from the sarcastic (nasty) utterances (Sec. 6);
4. Bootstrap this process on unannotated text to learn new extraction patterns to use for classification.

We show that the Extraction Pattern Learner improves the precision of our sarcasm classifier by 17% and the recall by 24%, and improves the precision of the nastiness classifier by 14% and recall by 13%. We discuss previous work in Sec. 2 and compare to ours in Sec. 7 where we also summarize our results and discuss future work.

## 2 Previous Work

IAC provides labels for sarcasm and nastiness that were collected with Mechanical Turk on Q/R pairs such as those in Fig. 1. Seven Turkers per Q/R pair answered a **binary** annotation question for sarcasm *Is the respondent using sarcasm?* (0,1) and a **scalar** annotation question for nastiness *Is the respondent attempting to be nice or is their attitude fairly nasty?* (-5 nasty ... 5 nice). We selected turns from IAC Table 1 with sarcasm averages above 0.5, and nasty averages below -1 and nice above 1. Fig. 1 included example nastiness and sarcasm values.

Previous work on the automatic identification of sarcasm has focused on Twitter using the `#sarcasm` (González-Ibáñez et al., 2011) and `#irony` (Reyes et al., 2012) tags and a combined variety of tags and smileys (Davidov et al., 2010). Another popular domain examines Amazon product reviews looking for irony (Reyes and Rosso, 2011), sarcasm (Tsur et al., 2010), and a corpus collection for sarcasm (Filatova, 2012). (Carvalho et al., 2009) looks for irony in comments in online newpapers which can have a thread-like structure. This primary focus on monologic venues suggests that sarcasm and irony can be detected with a relatively high precision but have a different structure from dialogues (Fox Tree and Schrock, 1999; Bryant and Fox Tree, 2002; Fox Tree, 2010), posing the question, can we generalize from monologic to dialogic structures? Each of these works use methods including LIWC unigrams, affect, polarity, punctuation and more, and achieve on average a precision of 75% or accuracy of between 45% and 85%.

Automatically identifying offensive utterances is also of interest. Previous work includes identifying flames in emails (Spertus, 1997) and other messaging interfaces (Razavi et al., 2010), identifying insults in Twitter (Xiang et al., 2012), as well as comments from new sites (Sood et al., 2011). These approaches achieve an accuracy between 64% and 83% using a variety of approaches. The accuracies for nasty utterances has a much smaller spread and higher average than sarcasm accuracies. This suggests that nasty language may be easier to identify than sarcastic language.

## 3 Method Overview

Our method for bootstrapping a classifier for sarcastic (nasty) dialogue acts uses R&W's model adapted to our data as illustrated for sarcasm in Fig. 2. The

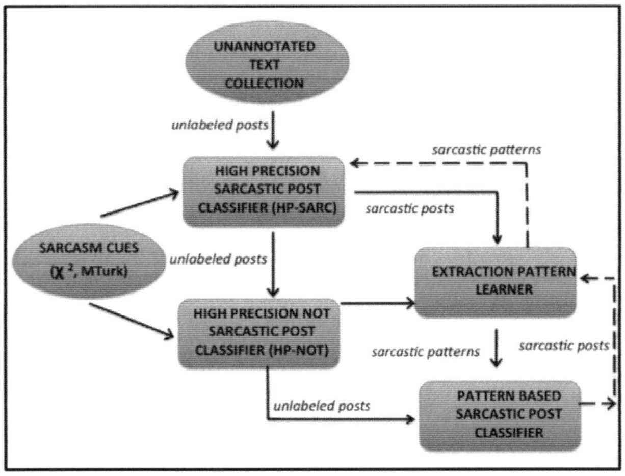


Figure 2: Bootstrapping Flow for Classifying Subjective Dialogue Acts, shown for sarcasm, but identical for nastiness.

| SARCASM | #sarc | #notsarc | total |
|---|---|---|---|
| MT exp dev | 617 | NA | 617 |
| HP train | 1407 | 1404 | 2811 |
| HP dev test | 1614 | 1614 | 3228 |
| PE eval | 1616 | 1616 | 3232 |
| All | 5254 | 4635 | 9889 |

| NASTY | #nasty | #nice | total |
|---|---|---|---|
| MT exp dev | 510 | NA | 510 |
| HP train | 1147 | 1147 | 2294 |
| HP dev test | 691 | 691 | 1382 |
| PE eval | 691 | 691 | 1382 |
| All | 3039 | 2529 | 5568 |

Table 1: How utterances annotated for sarcasm (top) and nastiness (bottom) in IAC were used. MT = Mechanical Turk experimental development set. HP train = utterances used to test whether combinations of cues could be used to develop a High precision classifier. HP dev test = "Unannotated Text Collection" in Fig. 2. PE eval = utterances used to train the Pattern Classifier.

overall idea of the method is to find reliable cues and then generalize. The top of Fig. 2 specifies the input to the method as an unannotated corpus of opinion dialogues, to illustrate the long term aim of building a large corpus of the phenomenon of interest without human annotation. Although the bootstrapping method assumes that the input is **unannotated text**, we first need utterances that are already labeled for sarcasm (nastiness) to train it. Table 1 specifies how we break down into datasets the annotations on the utterances in IAC for our various experiments.

The left circle of Fig. 2 reflects the assumption that there are Sarcasm or Nasty Cues that can identify the category of interest with high precision (R&W call this the "Known Subjective Vocabulary"). The aim of first developing a high precision classifier, at the expense of recall, is to select utterances that are reliably of the category of interest from unannotated text. This is needed to ensure that the generalization step of "Extraction Pattern Learner" does not introduce too much noise.

R&W did not need to develop a "Known Subjective Vocabulary" because previous work provided one (Wilson et al., 2005; Wiebe et al., 1999; Wiebe et al., 2003). Thus, our first question with applying R&W's method to our data was whether or not it is possible to develop a reliable set of Sarcasm (Nastiness) Cues (**O1** below). Two factors suggest that it might not be. First, R&W's method assumes that the cues are in the utterance to be classified, but it has been claimed that sarcasm (1) is context dependent, and (2) requires world knowledge to recognize, at least in many cases. Second, sarcasm is exhibited by a wide range of different forms and with different dialogue strategies such as jocularity, understatement and hyberbole (Gibbs, 2000; Eisterhold et al., 2006; Bryant and Fox Tree, 2002; Filatova, 2012). In Sec. 4 we devise and test two different methods for acquiring a set of Sarcasm (Nastiness) Cues on particular development sets of dialogue turns called the "MT exp dev" in Table 1.

The boxes labeled "High Precision Sarcastic Post Classifier" and "High Precision Not Sarcastic Post Classifier" in Fig. 2 involves using the Sarcasm (Nastiness) Cues in simple combinations that maximize precision at the expense of recall. R&W found cue combinations that yielded a High Precision Classifier (HP Classifier) with 90% precision and 32% recall on their dataset. We discuss our test of these steps in Sec. 5 on the "HP train" development sets in Table 1 to estimate parameters for the High Precision classifier, and then test the HP classifier with these parameters on the test dataset labeled "HP dev test" in Table 1.

R&W's Pattern Based classifier increased recall to 40% while losing very little precision. The open question with applying R&W's method to our data, was whether the cues that we discovered, by whatever method, would work at high enough precision to support generalization (**O2** below). In Sec. 6 we describe how we use the "PE eval" development set (Table 1) to estimate parameters for the Extraction Pattern Learner, and then test the Pattern Based Sarcastic (Nasty) Post classifier on the newly classified utterances from the dataset labeled "HP dev test" (Table 1). Our final open question was whether the extraction patterns from R&W, which worked well for news text, would work on social dialogue (**O3** below). Thus our experiments address the following open questions as to whether R&W's bootstrapping method improves classifiers for sarcasm and nastiness in online dialogues:

- (**O1**) Can we develop a "known sarcastic (nasty) vocabulary"? The LH circle of Fig. 2 illustrates that we use two different methods to identify **Sarcasm Cues**. Because we have utterances labeled as sarcastic, we compare a statistical method that extracts important features automatically from utterances, with a method that has a human in the loop, asking annotators to select phrases that are good indicators of sarcasm (nastiness) (Sec. 5);
- (**O2**) If we can develop a reliable set of sarcasm (nastiness) cues, is it then possible to develop an HP classifier? Will our precision be high enough? Is the fact that sarcasm is often context dependent an issue? (Sec. 5);
- (**O3**) Will the extraction patterns used in R&W's work allow us to generalize sarcasm cues from the HP Classifiers? Are R&W's patterns general enough to work well for dialogue and social language? (Sec. 6).

## 4 Sarcasm and Nastiness Cues

Because there is no prior "Known Sarcastic Vocabulary" we pilot two different methods for discovering lexical cues to sarcasm and nastiness, and experiment with combinations of cues that could yield a high precision classifier (Gianfortoni et al., 2011). The first method uses $\chi^2$ to measure whether a word or phrase is statistically indicative of sarcasm (nastiness) in the development sets labeled "MT exp dev" (Table 1). This method, a priori, seems reasonable because it is likely that if you have a large enough set of utterances labeled as sarcastic, you could be able to automatically learn a set of reliable cues for sarcasm.

The second method introduces a step of human annotation. We ask Turkers to identify sarcastic (nasty) indicators in utterances (the open question **O1**) from the development set "MT exp dev" (Table 1). Turkers were presented with utterances previously labeled sarcastic or nasty in IAC by 7 different Turkers, and were told "In a previous study, these responses were identified as being sarcastic by 3 out of 4 Turkers. For each quote/response pair, we will ask you to identify sarcastic or potentially sarcastic phrases in the response". The Turkers then selected words or phrases from the response they believed could lead someone to believing the utterance was sarcastic or nasty. These utterances were not used again in further experiments. This crowdsourcing method is similar to (Filatova, 2012), but where their data is monologic, ours is dialogic.

| **unigram** | | | |
|---|---|---|---|
| $\chi^2$ | MT | IA | FREQ |
| right | ah | .95 | 2 |
| oh | relevant | .85 | 2 |
| we | amazing | .80 | 2 |
| same | haha | .75 | 2 |
| all | yea | .73 | 3 |
| them | thanks | .68 | 6 |
| mean | oh | .56 | 56 |
| **bigram** | | | |
| $\chi^2$ | MT | IA | FREQ |
| the same | oh really | .83 | 2 |
| mean like | oh yeah | .79 | 2 |
| trying to | so sure | .75 | 2 |
| that you | no way | .72 | 3 |
| oh yeah | get real | .70 | 2 |
| I think | oh no | .66 | 4 |
| we should | you claim | .65 | 2 |
| **trigram** | | | |
| $\chi^2$ | MT | IA | FREQ |
| you mean to | I get it | .97 | 3 |
| mean to tell | I'm so sure | .65 | 2 |
| have to worry | then of course | .65 | 2 |
| sounds like a | are you saying | .60 | 2 |
| to deal with | well if you | .55 | 2 |
| I know I | go for it | .52 | 2 |
| you mean to | oh, sorry | .50 | 2 |

Table 2: Mechanical Turk (MT) and $\chi^2$ indicators for Sarcasm

### 4.1 Results from Indicator Cues

Sarcasm is known to be highly variable in form, and to depend, in some cases, on context for its interpretation (Sperber and Wilson, 1981; Gibbs, 2000; Bryant and Fox Tree, 2002). We conducted an initial pilot on 100 of the 617 sarcastic utterances in

| unigram | | | |
|---|---|---|---|
| $\chi^2$ | MT | IA | FREQ |
| like | idiot | .90 | 3 |
| them | unfounded | .85 | 2 |
| too | babbling | .80 | 2 |
| oh | lie | .72 | 11 |
| mean | selfish | .70 | 2 |
| just | nonsense | .69 | 9 |
| make | hurt | .67 | 3 |
| **bigram** | | | |
| $\chi^2$ | MT | IA | FREQ |
| of the | don't expect | .95 | 2 |
| you mean | get your | .90 | 2 |
| yes, | you're an | .85 | 2 |
| oh, | what's your | .77 | 4 |
| you are | prove it | .77 | 3 |
| like a | get real | .75 | 2 |
| I think | what else | .70 | 2 |
| **trigram** | | | |
| $\chi^2$ | MT | IA | FREQ |
| to tell me | get your sick | .75 | 2 |
| would deny a | your ignorance is | .70 | 2 |
| like that? | make up your | .70 | 2 |
| mean to tell | do you really | .70 | 2 |
| sounds like a | do you actually | .65 | 2 |
| you mean to | doesn't make it | .63 | 3 |
| to deal with | what's your point | .60 | 2 |

Table 3: Mechanical Turk (MT) and $\chi^2$ indicators for Nasty

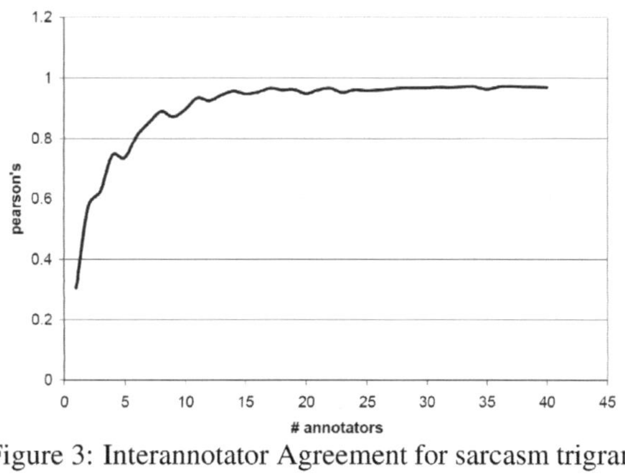

Figure 3: Interannotator Agreement for sarcasm trigrams

the development set "MT exp dev" to see if this was necessarily the case in our dialogues. (Snow et al., 2008) measures the quality of Mechanical Turk annotations on common NLP tasks by comparing them to a gold standard. Pearson's correlation coefficient shows that very few Mechanical Turk annotators were required to beat the gold standard data, often less than 5. Because our sarcasm task does not have gold standard data, we ask 100 annotators to participate in the pilot. Fig. 3 plots the average interannotator agreement (ITA) as a function of the number of annotators, computed using Pearson correlation counts, for 40 annotators and for trigrams which require more data to converge. In all cases (unigrams, bigrams, trigrams) ITA plateaus at around 20 annotators and is about 90% with 10 annotators, showing that the Mechanical Turk tasks are well formed and there is high agreement. Thus we elicited only 10 annotations for the remainder of the sarcastic and all the nasty utterances from the development set "MT exp dev".

We begin to form our "known sarcastic vocabulary" from these indicators, (open question **O1**). Each MT indicator has a **FREQ** (frequency): the number of times each indicator appears in the training set; and an **IA** (interannotator agreement): how many annotators agreed that each indicator was sarcastic or nasty. Table 2 shows the best unigrams, bigrams, and trigrams from the $\chi^2$ test and from the sarcasm Mechanical Turk experiment and Table 3 shows the results from the nasty experiment. We compare the MT indicators to the $\chi^2$ indicators as part of investigating open question **O1**.

As a pure statistical method, $\chi^2$ can pick out things humans might not. For example, if it just happened that the word 'we' only occurs in sarcastic utterances in the development set, then $\chi^2$ will select it as a strong sarcastic word (row 3 of Table 2). However, no human would recognize this word as corresponding to sarcasm. $\chi^2$ could easily be overtrained if the "MT exp dev" development set is not large enough to eliminate such general words from consideration, "MT exp dev" only has 617 sarcastic utterances and 510 nasty utterances (Table 1).

Words that the annotators select as indicators (columns labeled MT in Table 2 and Table 3) are much more easily identifiable although they do not appear as often. For example, the **IA** of 0.95 for 'ah' in Table 2 means that of all the annotators who saw 'ah' in the utterance they annotated, 95% selected it to be sarcastic. However the **FREQ** of 2 means that 'ah' only appeared in 2 utterances in the "MT exp dev" development set.

We test whether any of the methods for selecting indicators provide reliable cues that generalize to a larger dataset in Sec. 5. The parameters that we estimate on the development sets are exactly how frequent (compared to a $\theta_1$) and how reliable (compared to a $\theta_2$) a cue has to be to be useful in R&W's bootstrapping method.

## 5 High-Precision Classifiers

R&W use their "known subjective vocabulary" to train a High Precision classifier. R&W's HP classifier searches for exact surface matches of the subjective indicators and classifies utterances as subjective if two subjective indicators are present. We follow similar guidelines to train HP Sarcasm and Nasty Classifiers. To test open question **O1**, we use a development set called "HP train" (Table 1) to test three methods for measuring the "goodness" of an indicator that could serve as a high precision cue: (1) interannotator agreement based on annotators consensus from Mechanical Turk, on the assumption that the number of annotators that select a cue indicates its strength and reliability (*IA features*); (2) percent sarcastic (nasty) and frequency statistics in the HP train dataset as R&W do (*percent features*); and (3) the $\chi^2$ percent sarcastic (nasty) and frequency statistics ($\chi^2$ *features*).

The *IA features* use the MT indicators and the **IA** and **FREQ** calculations introduced in Sec. 4 (see Tables 2 and 3). First, we select indicators such that $\theta_1 <= \textbf{FREQ}$ where $\theta_1$ is a set of possible thresholds. Then we introduce two new parameters $\alpha$ and $\beta$ to divide the indicators into three "goodness" groups that reflect interannotator agreement.

$$indicatorstrength = \begin{cases} weak & if\ 0 \leq \textbf{IA} < \alpha \\ medium & if\ \alpha \leq \textbf{IA} < \beta \\ strong & if\ \beta \leq \textbf{IA} < 1 \end{cases}$$

For *IA features*, an utterance is classified as sarcastic if it contains at least one *strong* or two *medium* indicators. Other conditions were piloted. We first hypothesized that weak cues might be a way of classifying "not sarcastic" utterances. But HP train showed that both sarcastic and not sarcastic utterances contain weak indicators yielding no information gain. The same is true for Nasty's counter-class Nice. Thus we specify that counter-class utterances must have no *strong* indicators or at most one *medium* indicator. In contrast, R&W's counter-class classifier looks for a maximum of one subjective indicator.

The *percent features* also rely on the **FREQ** of each MT indicator, subject to a $\theta_1$ threshold, as well as the percentage of the time they occur in a sarcastic utterance (**%SARC**) or nasty utterance (**%NASTY**). We select indicators with various parameters for $\theta_1$ and $\theta_2 \leq$ **%SARC**. At least two indicators must be present and above the thresholds to be classified and we exhaust all combinations. Less than two indicators are needed to be classified as the counter-class, as in R&W.

Finally, the $\chi^2$ *features* use the same method as *percent features* only using the $\chi^2$ indicators instead of the MT indicators.

After determining which parameter settings performs the best for each feature set, we ran the HP classifiers, using each feature set and the best parameters, on the test set labeled "HP dev test". The HP Classifiers classify the utterances that it is confident on, and leave others unlabeled.

### 5.1 Results from High Precision Classifiers

The HP Sarcasm and Nasty Classifiers were trained on the three feature sets with the following parameters: *IA features* we exhaust all combinations of $\beta =$ [.70, .75, .80, .85, .90, .95, 1.00], $\alpha =$ [.35, .40, .45, .50, .55, .60, .65, .7], and $\theta_1 =$ [2, 4, 6, 8, 10]; for the *percent features* and $\chi^2$ *features* we again exhaust $\theta_1$ = [2, 4, 6, 8, 10] and $\theta_2 =$ [.55, .60, .65, .70, .75, .80, .85, .90, .95, 1.00].

Tables 4 and 5 show a subset of the experiments with each feature set. We want to select parameters that maximize precision without sacrificing too much recall. Of course, the parameters that yield the highest precision also have the lowest recall, e.g. Sarcasm *percent features*, parameters $\theta_1 = 4$ and $\theta_2 = 0.75$ achieve 92% precision but the recall is 1% (Table 4), and Nasty *percent features* with parameters $\theta_1 = 8$ and $\theta_2 = 0.8$ achieves 98% precision but a recall of 3% (Table 5). On the other end of the spectrum, the parameters that achieve the highest recall yield a precision equivalent to random chance.

Examining the parameter combinations in Tables 4 and 5 shows that *percent features* do better than *IA features* in all cases in terms of precision. Compare the block of results labeled % in Tables 4 and 5 with the IA and $\chi^2$ blocks for column P. Nasty appears to be easier to identify than Sarcasm, especially using the *percent features*. The performance of the $\chi^2$ *features* is comparable to that of *percent features* for sarcasm, but lower than *percent features* for Nasty.

The best parameters selected from each feature set are shown in the PARAMS column of Table 6. With the indicators learned from these parameters, we run the Classifiers on the test set labeled "HP

| SARC | PARAMS | P | R | N (tp) |
|---|---|---|---|---|
| % | $\theta_1$ =4, $\theta_2$ =.55 | 62% | 55% | 768 |
| | 4, .6 | 72% | 32% | 458 |
| | 4, .65 | 84% | 12% | 170 |
| | 4, .75 | 92% | 1% | 23 |
| IA | $\theta_1$ =2, $\beta$ =.90, $\alpha$ =.35 | 51% | 73% | 1,026 |
| | 2, .95, .55 | 62% | 13% | 189 |
| | 2, .9, .55 | 54% | 34% | 472 |
| | 4, .75, .5 | 64% | 7% | 102 |
| | 4, .75, .6 | 78% | 1% | 22 |
| $\chi^2$ | $\theta_1$ =8, $\theta_2$ =.55 | 59% | 64% | 893 |
| | 8, .6 | 67% | 31% | 434 |
| | 8, .65 | 70% | 12% | 170 |
| | 8, .75 | 93% | 1% | 14 |

Table 4: Sarcasm Train results; P: precision, R: recall, tp: true positive classifications

| NASTY | PARAMS | P | R | N (tp) |
|---|---|---|---|---|
| % | $\theta_1$ =2, $\theta_2$ =.55 | 65% | 69% | 798 |
| | 4, .65 | 80% | 44% | 509 |
| | 8, .75 | 95% | 11% | 125 |
| | 8, .8 | 98% | 3% | 45 |
| IA | $\theta_1$ =2, $\beta$ =.95, $\alpha$ =.35 | 50% | 96% | 1,126 |
| | 2, .95, .45 | 60% | 59% | 693 |
| | 4, .75, .45 | 60% | 50% | 580 |
| | 2, .7, .55 | 73% | 12% | 149 |
| | 2, .9, .65 | 85% | 1% | 17 |
| $\chi^2$ | $\theta_1$ =2, $\theta_2$ =.55 | 73% | 15% | 187 |
| | 2, .65 | 78% | 8% | 104 |
| | 2, .7 | 86% | 3% | 32 |

Table 5: Nasty Train results; P: precision, R: recall, tp: true positive classifications

dev test" (Table 1). The performance on test set "HP dev test" (Table 6) is worse than on the training set (Tables 4 and 5). However we conclude that **both the % and $\chi^2$ features** provide candidates for sarcasm (nastiness) cues that are high enough precision (open question **O2**) to be used in the Extraction Pattern Learner (Sec. 6), even if Sarcasm is more context dependent than Nastiness.

| | PARAMS | P | R | F |
|---|---|---|---|---|
| Sarc % | $\theta_1$ =4, $\theta_2$ =.55 | 54% | 38% | 0.46 |
| Sarc IA | $\theta_1$ =2, $\beta$ =.95, $\alpha$ =.55 | 56% | 11% | 0.34 |
| Sarc $\chi^2$ | $\theta_1$ =8, $\theta_2$ =.60 | 60% | 19% | 0.40 |
| Nasty % | $\theta_1$ =2, $\theta_2$ =.55 | 58% | 49% | 0.54 |
| Nasty IA | $\theta_1$ =2, $\beta$ =.95, $\alpha$ =.45 | 53% | 35% | 0.44 |
| Nasty $\chi^2$ | $\theta_1$ =2, $\theta_2$ =.55 | 74% | 14% | 0.44 |

Table 6: HP Dev test results; PARAMS: the best parameters for each feature set P: precision, R: recall, F: f-measure

## 6 Extraction Patterns

R&W's Pattern Extractor searches for instances of the 13 templates in the first column of Table 7 in utterances classified by the HP Classifier. We reimplement this; an example of each pattern as instantiated in test set "HP dev test" for our data is shown in the second column of Table 7. The template <subj> active-verb <dobj> matches utterances where a subject is followed by an active verb and a direct object. However, these matches are not limited to exact surface matches as the HP Classifiers required, e.g. this pattern would match the phrase "have a problem". Table 10 in the Appendix provides example utterances from IAC that match the instantiated template patterns. For example, the excerpt from the first row in Table 10 "It is quite strange to encounter someone in this day and age who lacks any knowledge whatsoever of the mechanism of adaptation since it **was explained** 150 years ago" matches the <subj> passive-verb pattern. It appears 2 times (**FREQ**) in the test set and is sarcastic both times (**%SARC** is 100%). Row 11 in Table 10 shows an utterance matching the active-verb prep <np> pattern with the phrase "At the time of the Constitution there weren't exactly vast suburbs that could be prowled by thieves **looking for** an open window". This phrase appears 14 times (**FREQ**) in the test set and is sarcastic (**%SARC**) 92% of the time it appears.

| Synactic Form | Example Pattern |
|---|---|
| <subj> passive-verb | <subj> was explained |
| <subj> active-verb | <subj> appears |
| <subj> active-verb dobj | <subj> have problem |
| <subj> verb infinitive | <subj> have to do |
| <subj> aux noun | <subj> is nothing |
| active-verb <dobj> | gives <dobj> |
| infinitive <dobj> | to force <dobj> |
| verb infinitive <dobj> | want to take <dobj> |
| noun aux <dobj> | fact is <dobj> |
| noun prep <np> | argument against <np> |
| active-verb prep <np> | looking for <np> |
| passive-verb prep <np> | was put in <np> |
| infinitive prep <np> | to go to <np> |

Table 7: Syntactic Templates and Examples of Patterns that were Learned for Sarcasm. Table. 10 in the Appendix provides example posts that instantiate these patterns.

The Pattern Based Classifiers are trained on a development set labeled "PE eval" (Table 1). Utterances from this development set are not used again

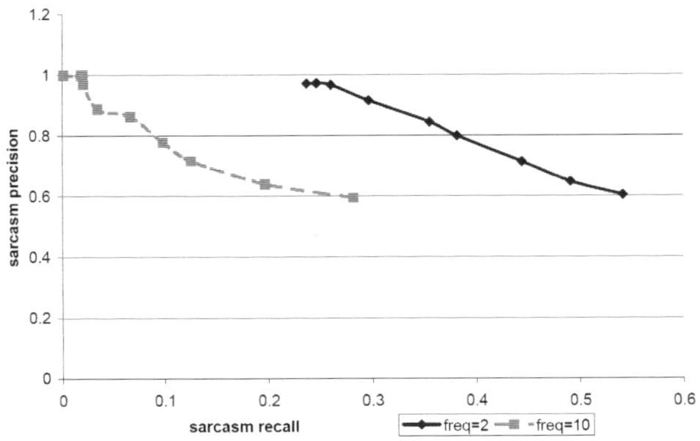


Figure 4: Recall vs. Precision for Sarcasm PE eval

in any further experiments. Patterns are extracted from the dataset and we again compute **FREQ** and **%SARC** and **%NASTY** for each pattern subject to $\theta_1 \leq$ **FREQ** and $\theta_2 \leq$ **%SARC** or **% NASTY**. Classifications are made if at least two patterns are present and both are above the specified $\theta_1$ and $\theta_2$, as in R&W. Also following R&W, we do not learn "not sarcastic" or "nice" patterns.

To test the Pattern Based Classifiers, we use as input the classifications made by the HP Classifiers. Using the predicted labels from the classifiers as the true labels, the patterns from test set "HP test dev" are extracted and compared to those patterns found in development set "PE eval". We have two feature sets for both sarcasm and nastiness: one using the predictions from the MT indicators in the HP classifier (*percent features*) and another using those instances from the $\chi^2$ *features*.

### 6.1 Results from Pattern Classifier

The Pattern Classifiers classify an utterance as Sarcastic (Nasty) if at least two patterns are present and above the thresholds $\theta_1$ and $\theta_2$, exhausting all combinations of $\theta_1$ = [2, 4, 6, 8, 10] and $\theta_2$ = [.55, .60, .65, .70, .75, .80, .85, .90, .95, 1.00]. The counter-classes are predicted when the utterance contains less than two patterns. The exhaustive classifications are first made using the utterances in the development set labeled "PE eval". Fig. 4 shows the precision and recall trade-off for $\theta_1$ = [2, 10] and all $\theta_2$ values on sarcasm development set"PE eval". As recall increases, precision drops. By including patterns that only appear 2 times, we get better recall. Limiting $\theta_1$ to 10 yields fewer patterns and lower recall.

Table 8 shows the results for various parameters. The PE dev dataset learned a total of 1,896 sarcastic extraction patterns above a minimum threshold of $\theta_1 < 2$ and $\theta_2 < 0.55$, and similarly 847 nasty extraction patterns. Training on development set "PE dev" yields high precision and good recall. To select the best parameters, we again look for a balance between precision and recall. Both Classifiers have very high precision. In the end, we select parameters that have a better recall than the best parameter from the HP Classifiers which is $recall = 38\%$ for sarcasm and $recall = 49\%$ for nastiness. The best parameters and their test results are shown in Table 9.

| | PARAMS | P | R | F | N (tp) |
|---|---|---|---|---|---|
| SARC | $\theta_1$ =2, $\theta_2$ =.60 | 65% | 49% | 0.57 | 792 |
| | 2, .65 | 71% | 44% | 0.58 | 717 |
| | 2, .70 | 80% | 38% | 0.59 | 616 |
| | 2, 1.0 | 97% | 24% | 0.60 | 382 |
| NASTY | $\theta_1$ =2, $\theta_2$ =.65 | 71% | 49% | 0.60 | 335 |
| | 2, .75 | 83% | 42% | 0.62 | 289 |
| | 2, .90 | 96% | 30% | 0.63 | 209 |

Table 8: Pattern Classification Training; P: precision, R: recall, F: F-measure, tp: true positive classifications

The Pattern Classifiers are tested on "HP dev test" with the labels predicted by our HP Classifiers, thus we have two different sets of classifications for both Sarcasm and Nastiness: *percent features* and $\chi^2$ *features*. Overall, the Pattern Classification performs better on Nasty than Sarcasm. Also, the *percent features* yield better results than $\chi^2$ features, possibly because the precision for $\chi^2$ is high from the HP Classifiers, but the recall is very low. We believe that $\chi^2$ selects statistically predictive indicators that are tuned to the dataset, rather than general. Having **a human in the loop guarantees more general features** from a smaller dataset. Whether this remains true on the size as the dataset increases to 1000 or more is unknown. We conclude that R&W's patterns generalize well on our Sarcasm and Nasty datasets (open question **O3**), but suspect that there may be better syntactic patterns for bootstrapping sarcasm and nastiness, e.g. involving cue words or semantic categories of words rather than syntactic categories, as we discuss in Sec. 7.

This process can be repeated by taking the newly classified utterances from the Pattern Based Classifiers, then applying the Pattern Extractor to learn new patterns from the newly classified data. This

| | PARAMS | P | R | F |
|---|---|---|---|---|
| Sarc % | $\theta_1$ =2, $\theta_2$ =.70 | 62% | 52% | 0.57 |
| Sarc $\chi^2$ | $\theta_1$ =2, $\theta_2$ =.70 | 31% | 58% | 0.45 |
| Nasty % | $\theta_1$ =2, $\theta_2$ =.65 | 75% | 62% | 0.69 |
| Nasty $\chi^2$ | $\theta_1$ =2, $\theta_2$ =.65 | 30% | 70% | 0.50 |

Table 9: The results for Pattern Classification on HP dev test dataset ; PARAMS: the best parameters for each feature set P: precision, R: recall, F: f-measure

can be repeated for multiple iterations. We leave this for future work.

## 7 Discussion and Future Work

In this work, we apply a bootstrapping method to train classifiers to identify particular types of subjective utterances in online dialogues. First we create a suite of linguistic indicators for sarcasm and nastiness using crowdsourcing techniques. Our crowdsourcing method is similar to (Filatova, 2012). From these new linguistic indicators we construct a classifier following previous work on bootstrapping subjectivity classifiers (Riloff and Wiebe, 2003; Thelen and Riloff, 2002). We compare the performance of the High Precision Classifier that was trained based on statistical measures against one that keeps human annotators in the loop, and find that Classifiers using statistically selected indicators appear to be overtrained on the development set because they do not generalize well. This first phase achieves 54% precision and 38% recall for sarcastic utterances using the human selected indicators. If we bootstrap by using syntactic patterns to create more general sarcasm indicators from the utterances identified as sarcastic in the first phase, we achieve a higher precision of 62% and recall of 52%.

We apply the same method to bootstrapping a classifier for nastiness dialogic acts. Our first phase, using crowdsourced nasty indicators, achieves 58% precision and 49% recall, which increases to 75% precision and 62% recall when we bootstrap with syntactic patterns, possibly suggesting that nastiness (insults) are less nuanced and easier to detect than sarcasm.

Previous work claims that recognition of sarcasm (1) depends on knowledge of the speaker, (2) world knowledge, or (3) use of context (Gibbs, 2000; Eisterhold et al., 2006; Bryant and Fox Tree, 2002; Carvalho et al., 2009). While we also believe that certain types of subjective language cannot be determined from cue words alone, our Pattern Based Classifiers, based on syntactic patterns, still achieves high precision and recall. In comparison to previous monologic works whose sarcasm precision is about 75%, ours is not quite as good with 62%. While the nasty works do not report precision, we believe that they are comparable to the 64% - 83% accuracy with our precision of 75%.

Open question **O3** was whether R&W's patterns are fine tuned to subjective utterances in news. However R&W's patterns improve both precision and recall of our Sarcastic and Nasty classifiers. In future work however, we would like to test whether semantic categories of words rather than syntactic categories would perform even better for our problem, e.g. Linguistic Inquiry and Word Count categories. Looking again at row 1 in Table 10, "It is quite strange to encounter someone in this day and age who lacks any knowledge whatsoever of the mechanism of adaptation since it was explained 150 years ago", the word 'quite' matches the 'cogmech' and 'tentative' categories, which might be interesting to generalize to sarcasm. In row 11 "At the time of the Constitution there weren't exactly vast suburbs that could be prowled by thieves looking for an open window", the phrase "weren't exactly" could also match the LIWC categories 'cogmech' and 'certain' or, more specifically, certainty negated.

We also plan to extend this work to other categories of subjective dialogue acts, e.g. emotional and respectful as mentioned in the Introduction, and to expand our corpus of subjective dialogue acts. We will experiment with performing more than one iteration of the bootstrapping process (R&W complete two iterations) as well as create a Hybrid Classifier combining the subjective cues and patterns into a single Classifier that itself can be bootstrapped.

Finally, we would like to extend our method to different dialogue domains to see if the classifiers trained on our sarcastic and nasty indicators would achieve similar results or if different social media sites have their own style of displaying sarcasm or nastiness not comparable to those in forum debates.

## References

G.A. Bryant and J.E. Fox Tree. 2002. Recognizing verbal irony in spontaneous speech. *Metaphor and symbol*, 17(2):99–119.

P. Carvalho, L. Sarmento, M.J. Silva, and E. de Oliveira. 2009. Clues for detecting irony in user-generated contents: oh...!! it's so easy;-). In *Proc. of the 1st international CIKM workshop on Topic-sentiment analysis for mass opinion*, p. 53–56. ACM.

D. Davidov, O. Tsur, and A. Rappoport. 2010. Semi-supervised recognition of sarcastic sentences in twitter and amazon. In *Proc. of the Fourteenth Conference on Computational Natural Language Learning*, p. 107–116. Association for Computational Linguistics.

J. Eisterhold, S. Attardo, and D. Boxer. 2006. Reactions to irony in discourse: Evidence for the least disruption principle. *Journal of Pragmatics*, 38(8):1239–1256.

E. Filatova. 2012. Irony and sarcasm: Corpus generation and analysis using crowdsourcing. In *Language Resources and Evaluation Conference, LREC2012*.

J.E. Fox Tree and J.C. Schrock. 1999. Discourse Markers in Spontaneous Speech: Oh What a Difference an Oh Makes. *Journal of Memory and Language*, 40(2):280–295.

J. E. Fox Tree. 2010. Discourse markers across speakers and settings. *Language and Linguistics Compass*, 3(1):1–13.

P. Gianfortoni, D. Adamson, and C.P. Rosé. 2011. Modeling of stylistic variation in social media with stretchy patterns. In *Proc. of the First Workshop on Algorithms and Resources for Modelling of Dialects and Language Varieties*, p. 49–59. ACL.

R.W. Gibbs. 2000. Irony in talk among friends. *Metaphor and Symbol*, 15(1):5–27.

R. González-Ibáñez, S. Muresan, and N. Wacholder. 2011. Identifying sarcasm in twitter: a closer look. In *Proc. of the 49th Annual Meeting of the ACL: Human Language Technologies: short papers*, volume 2, p. 581–586.

A. Razavi, D. Inkpen, S. Uritsky, and S. Matwin. 2010. Offensive language detection using multi-level classification. *Advances in Artificial Intelligence*, p. 16–27.

A. Reyes and P. Rosso. 2011. Mining subjective knowledge from customer reviews: a specific case of irony detection. In *Proc. of the 2nd Workshop on Computational Approaches to Subjectivity and Sentiment Analysis (WASSA 2.011), ACL*, p. 118–124.

A. Reyes, P. Rosso, and D. Buscaldi. 2012. From humor recognition to irony detection: The figurative language of social media. *Data & Knowledge Engineering*.

E. Riloff and J. Wiebe. 2003. Learning extraction patterns for subjective expressions. In *Proc. of the 2003 conference on Empirical methods in Natural Language Processing-V. 10*, p. 105–112. ACL.

R. Snow, B. O'Conner, D. Jurafsky, and A.Y. Ng. 2008. Cheap and fast—but is it good?: evaluating non-expert annotations for natural language tasks In *Proc. of the Conference on Empirical Methods in Natural Language Processing*, p. 254–263. ACM.

S.O. Sood, E.F. Churchill, and J. Antin. 2011. Automatic identification of personal insults on social news sites. *Journal of the American Society for Information Science and Technology*.

Dan Sperber and Deidre Wilson. 1981. Irony and the use-mention distinction. In Peter Cole, editor, *Radical Pragmatics*, p. 295–318. Academic Press, N.Y.

E. Spertus. 1997. Smokey: Automatic recognition of hostile messages. In *Proc. of the National Conference on Artificial Intelligence*, p. 1058–1065.

M. Thelen and E. Riloff. 2002. A bootstrapping method for learning semantic lexicons using extraction pattern contexts. In *Proc. of the ACL-02 conference on Empirical methods in natural language processing-Volume 10*, p. 214–221. ACL.

O. Tsur, D. Davidov, and A. Rappoport. 2010. Icwsm–a great catchy name: Semi-supervised recognition of sarcastic sentences in online product reviews. In *Proc. of the fourth international AAAI conference on weblogs and social media*, p. 162–169.

Marilyn Walker, Pranav Anand, , Robert Abbott, and Jean E. Fox Tree. 2012. A corpus for research on deliberation and debate. In *Language Resources and Evaluation Conference, LREC2012*.

J.M. Wiebe, R.F. Bruce, and T.P. O'Hara. 1999. Development and use of a gold-standard data set for subjectivity classifications. In *Proc. of the 37th annual meeting of the Association for Computational Linguistics*, p. 246–253. ACL.

J. Wiebe, E. Breck, C. Buckley, C. Cardie, P. Davis, B. Fraser, D. Litman, D. Pierce, E. Riloff, T. Wilson, et al. 2003. Recognizing and organizing opinions expressed in the world press. In *Working Notes-New Directions in Question Answering (AAAI Spring Symposium Series)*.

T. Wilson, P. Hoffmann, S. Somasundaran, J. Kessler, J. Wiebe, Y. Choi, C. Cardie, E. Riloff, and S. Patwardhan. 2005. Opinionfinder: A system for subjectivity analysis. In *Proc. of HLT/EMNLP on Interactive Demonstrations*, p. 34–35. ACL.

G. Xiang, B. Fan, L. Wang, J. Hong, and C. Rose. 2012. Detecting offensive tweets via topical feature discovery over a large scale twitter corpus. In *Proc. of the 21st ACM international conference on Information and knowledge management*, p. 1980–1984. ACM.

## 8 Appendix A. Instances of Learned Patterns

| Pattern Instance | FREQ | %SARC | Example Utterance |
|---|---|---|---|
| `<subj> was explained` | 2 | 100% | Well, I incorrectly assumed that anyone attempting to enter the discussion would at least have a grasp of the most fundamental principles. It is quite strange to encounter someone in this day and age who lacks any knowledge whatsoever of the mechanism of adaptation since it **was explained** 150 years ago. |
| `<subj> appears` | 1 | 94% | It **appears** this thread has been attacked by the "line item " poster. |
| `<subj> have problem` | 4 | 50% | I see your point, Iangb but I'm not about to be leaving before you've had a chance to respond. I won't be "leaving " at all. You challenged me to produce an argument, so I'm going to produce my argument. I will then summarize the argument, and you can respond to it and we can then discuss / debate those specifics that you **have a problem** with. |
| `<subj> have to do` | 15 | 86% | How does purchasing a house **have to do** with abortion? Ok, so what if the kid wants to have the baby and the adults want to get rid of it? What if the adults want her to have the baby and the kid wants to get rid of it? You would force the kid to have a child (that doesn't seem responsible at all), or you would force the kid to abort her child (thereby taking away her son or daughter). Both of those decisions don't sound very consitent or responsible. The decision is best left up to the person that is pregnant, regardless of their age. |
| `<subj> is nothing` | 10 | 90% | Even though there **is nothing** but ad hoc answers to the questions, creationists touted the book as "proof " that Noahś ark was possible. They never seem to notice that no one has ever tried to build and float an ark. They prefer to put the money into creation museums and amusement parks. |
| `gives <dobj>` | 25 | 88% | Just knowing that there are many Senators and Congressmen who would like to abolish gun rights **gives** credence to the fact that government could actually try to limit or ban the 2nd Amendment in the future. |
| `to force <dobj>` | 9 | 89% | And I just say that it would be unjust and unfair of you **to force** metaphysical belief systems of your own which constitute religious belief upon your follows who may believe otherwise than you. Get pregnant and treat your fetus as a full person if you wish, nobody will force you to abort it. Let others follow their own beliefs differing or the same. Otherwise you attempt to obtain justice by doing injustice |
| `want to take <dobj>` | 5 | 80% | How far do you **want to take** the preemptive strike thing? Should we make it illegal for people to gather in public in groups of two or larger because anything else might be considered a violent mob assembly for the basis of creating terror and chaos? |
| `fact is <dobj>` | 6 | 83% | No, the **fact is** PP was founded by an avowed racist and staunch supporter of Eugenics. |
| `argument against <np>` | 4 | 75% | Perhaps I am too attached to this particular debate that you are having but if you actually have a sensible **argument against** gay marriage then please give it your best shot here. I look forward to reading your comments. |
| `looking for <np>` | 14 | 92% | At the time of the Constitution there weren't exactly vast suburbs that could be prowled by thieves **looking for** an open window. |
| `was put in <np>` | 3 | 66% | You got it wrong Daewoo. The ban **was put in** place by the 1986 Firearm Owners Protection Act, designed to correct the erronius Gun Control Act of 1968. The machinegun ban provision was slipped in at the last minute, during a time when those that would oppose it werenť there to debate it. |
| `to go to <np>` | 8 | 63% | Yes that would solve the problem wouldn't it,worked the first time around,I say that because we (U.S.)are compared to the wild west. But be they whites,Blacks,Reds,or pi** purple shoot a few that try to detain or threaten you, yeah I think they will back off unless they are prepared **to go to** war. |

Table 10: Sarcastic patterns and example instances

# Topical Positioning: A New Method for Predicting Opinion Changes in Conversation

**Ching-Sheng Lin[1], Samira Shaikh[1], Jennifer Stromer-Galley[1,2], Jennifer Crowley[1], Tomek Strzalkowski[1,3], Veena Ravishankar[1]**

[1]State University of New York - University at Albany, NY 12222 USA
[2]Syracuse University
[3]Polish Academy of Sciences
clin3@albany.edu, sshaikh@albany.edu, tomek@albany.edu

## Abstract

In this paper, we describe a novel approach to automatically detecting and tracking discussion dynamics in Internet social media by focusing on attitude modeling of topics. We characterize each participant's attitude towards topics as Topical Positioning, employ Topical Positioning Map to represent the positions of participants with respect to each other and track attitude shifts over time. We also discuss how we used participants' attitudes towards system-detected meso-topics to reflect their attitudes towards the overall topic of conversation. Our approach can work across different types of social media, such as Twitter discussion and online chat room. In this article, we show results on Twitter data.

## 1 Introduction

The popularity of social networks and the new kinds of communication they support provides never before available opportunities to examine people behaviors, ideas, and sentiments in various forms of interaction. One of the active research subjects is to automatically identify sentiment, which has been adopted in many different applications such as text summarization and product review. In general, people express their stances and rationalize their thoughts on the topics in social media discussion platform. Moreover, some of them explicitly or implicitly establish strategies to persuade others to embrace his/her belief. For example, in the discussion of the topic "Should the legal drinking age be lowered to 18", the participants who are against it may state their views explicitly and list negative consequences of lowering drinking age to 18 in an attempt to change opinions of those who appear to support the change. This phenomenon actually involves two research problems which have been of great interest in Natural Language Processing: opinion identification and sociolinguistic modeling of discourse. The first problem can be addressed by traditional opinion analysis that recognizes which position or stance a person is taking for the given topics (Somasundaran and Wiebe, 2009). The second part requires modeling the sociolinguistic aspects of interactions between participants to detect more subtle opinion shifts that may be revealed by changes in interpersonal conversational dynamics. In this paper, we bring these two research avenues together and describe a prototype automated system that: (1) discovers each participant's position polarities with respect to various topics in conversation, (2) models how participants' positions change over the course of conversation, and (3) measures the distances between participants' relative positions on all topics. We analyzed discussions on Twitter to construct a set of meso-topics based on the persistence of certain noun phrases and co-referential expressions used by the participants. A meso-topic is any local topic in conversation referred to by a noun phrase and subsequently mentioned again at least 5 times via repetition, pronoun or synonym. Meso-topics do not necessarily represent actual topics of conversations, but certainly are important interactive handles used by the speakers. It is our hypothesis that meso-topics can be effectively used to track and predict polarity changes in speakers' positions towards the overall topic of conversation. Once the meso-topics and their polarities for each participant are determined, we can generate a *topical positioning map (or network)* (TPN) showing relative distances between participants based on all meso-topics in discourse. Comparing different snapshots of the TPN over time, we can observe how the group's dynamic changes, i.e., how some participants move closer to one another while others drift apart in the discussion. In particular, we suggest that TPN changes can track and predict participants' changes of opinion about the overall topic of conversation.

The remainder of this paper is organized as follows. In Section 2, we review related work. In Section 3, we describe the components of the proposed technique and the way they are used to implement the system. In Section 4, we discuss initial empirical studies, including data collection and evaluation. In final section, we present conclusions and some future work.

## 2 Related Work

While systematic research on opinion tracking and influence in dialogues is a relatively new area of computational linguistics, related research includes automatic opinion mining and sentiments extraction from text (Wiebe et al., 2005; Strapparava and Mihalcea, 2008), speech (Vogt et al., 2008) and social networking sites (Martineau and Finin, 2009). Much of the recent work was focused on automatic analysis of product reviews (books, movies, etc.) and extracting customers' opinions from them (Hu and Liu, 2004; David and Pinch, 2006; Zhuang et al., 2006). A typical approach is to count the number of 'opinion' words within a text window around the product names, possibly augmented with syntactic parsing to get dependencies right. An opinion mining application can extract either full opinion sentences (Philip et al., 2003) or may generate a more structured representation (Hu and Liu, 2004). Another recent application of sentiment analysis is ECO system (Effective Communication Online) (Small et al., 2010) that constructs a model of a community-wide sentiment towards certain common issues discussed in social media, particularly forums and open blogs. This model is then used to assess whether a new post would fit into the targeted community by comparing the sentiment polarities about the concepts in the message and in the model. Potential posters are then guided in ways to shape their communication so that it minimizes the number of conflicting concept sentiments, while still preserving the intended message.

Another related research domain is about modeling the social phenomena in discourse. (Strzalkowski et al., 2010, Broadwell et al., 2012) proposed a two-tier approach that relies on extracting observable linguistic features of conversational text to detect mid-level social behaviors such as Topic Control, Disagreement and Involvement. These social behaviors are then used to infer higher-level social roles such as Leader and Influencer, which may have impact on how other participants' opinions form and change.

## 3 System Modules

In this section, we describe a series of modules in our system, which include meso-topic extraction, topical positioning and topical positioning map, and explain how we capture opinion shifts.

### 3.1 Meso-Topic Extraction

Participants mention many ideas and subjects in dialogue. We call these Local Topics, which are any noun phrases introduced that are subsequently mentioned via repetition, synonym, or pronoun (Strzalkowski et al., 2010) by the same participant or different participants. Some local topics persist for only a couple of turns, others for much longer; some are closely relevant to the overall discussion, while others may appear to be digressions. We identify local topics, their first mentions and subsequent mentions, and track participants who make these mentions. Once local topics have been introduced into the dialogue we track their persistence as topic chains, through repetitions of the noun phrase as well as references via pronouns and the use of synonyms. Topic chains do not have to be continuous, they may contain gaps. The lengths of these gaps are also important to measures for some behaviors. Meso-topics are the most persistent local topics, topics that are widely cited through long stretches of discourse. A selection of meso-topics is closely associated with the task in which the discourse participants are engaged. Short "gaps" in the chain are permitted (up to 10 turns, to accommodate digressions, obscure references, noise, etc.). Meso-topics can be distinguished from the local topics because the participants often make polarized statements about them. We use the Stanford part-of-speech tagger (Klein and Manning, 2003) to automatically detect nouns and noun phrases in dialogue and select those with subsequent mentions as local topics using a fairly simple pronoun resolution method based primarily on presence of specific lexical features as well as temporal distance between utterances. Princeton Wordnet (Fellbaum et al., 2006) is consulted to identify synonyms and other related words commonly used in co-references. The local topics that form sufficiently long co-reference chains are designated as meso-topics.

### 3.2 Topical Positioning

Topical Positioning is defined as the attitude a speaker has towards the meso-topics of discussion. Speakers in a dialogue, when discussing issues, especially ones with some controversy, will establish their attitude on each topic, classified as for, against, or neutral/undecided. In so doing, they establish their positions on the issue or topic, which shapes the agenda of the discussion and also shapes the outcomes or conclusions of the discussion. Characterizing topical positioning allows us to see the speakers who are for, who are against, and who are neutral/undecided on a given topic or issue.

To establish topical positioning, we first identify meso-topics that are present in a discourse. For each utterance made by a speaker on a meso-topic we then establish its polarity, i.e., if this utterance is 'for' (positive) or 'against' (negative), or neutral on the topic. We distinguish three forms of meso-topic valuation that may be present: (a) *express advocacy/disadvocacy*, when the valuation is applied directly to the topic (e.g., "I'm for Carla"); (b) *supporting/dissenting information*, when the valuation is made indirectly by offering additional information about the topic (e.g., "He's got experience with youngsters."); and (c) express agreement/disagreement with a polarized statement made by another speaker.

The following measures of Topical Positioning are defined: Topic Polarity Index, which establishes the polarity of a speaker's attitude towards the topic, and Polarity Strength Index, which measures the magnitude of this attitude.

[*Topic Polarity Index (TPX)*] In order to detect the polarity of Topical Positioning on meso-topic T, we count for each speaker:

- All utterances on T using statements with polarity P applied directly to T using appropriate adverb or adjective phrases, or when T is a direct object of a verb. Polarities of adjectives and adverbs are taken from the expanded ANEW lexicon (Bradley and Lang, 1999).
- All utterances that offer information with polarity P about topic T.
- All responses to other speakers' statements with polarity P applied to T. In the Twitter environment (and the like), for now we include a re-tweet in this category.

Given these counts we can calculate TPX for each speaker as a proportion of positive, negative and neutral polarity utterances made by this speaker about topic T. A speaker whose utterances are overwhelmingly positive (80% or more) has a pro-topic position (TPX = +1); a speaker whose utterances are overwhelmingly negative takes an against-topic position (TPX = –1); a speaker whose utterances are largely neutral or whose utterances vary in polarity, has a neutral/undecided position on the topic (TPX = 0).

[*Polarity Strength Index (PSX)*] In addition to the valence of the Topical Positioning, we also wish to calculate its strength. To do so, we calculate the proportion of utterances on the topic made by each speaker to all utterances made about this topic by all speakers in the discourse. Speakers, who make most utterances on the topic relative to other speakers, take a stronger position on this topic. PSX is measured on a 5-point scale corresponding to the quintiles in normal distribution.

*Topical Positioning Measure (TPM)*
In order to establish the value of Topical Positioning for a given topic we combine the values of TPX*PSX. Topical Positioning takes values between +5 (strongest pro) to 0 (neutral/undecided) to –5 (strongest against). For example, a speaker who makes 25% of all utterances on the topic "Carla" (group mean is 12%) and whose most statements are positive, has the strongest pro Topical Positioning on Carla: +5 (for fifth quintile on the positive side).

### 3.3 Topical Positioning Map (TPN)

Given the combined values of TPM for each participant in a group, we can calculate distances between the speakers on each meso-topic as well as on all meso-topics in a conversation. For meso-topics (t1, ... tN), the distance is calculated using a cosine between speakers' "vectors" ($TPM_{t1}(A)$ ... $TPM_{tN}(A)$) and ($TPM_{t1}(B)$ ... $TPM_{tN}(B)$). Specifically, we use *(1-Cosine(V1, V2))* to represent distance between node V1 and V2 in the network, where the range becomes 0 to 2.

With the aid of TPN, we can detect the opinion shifts and model the impact of speakers with specific social roles in the group, which in our case is the influencer. An influencer is a group participant who has credibility in the group and introduces ideas that others pick up on or support. An influencer model is generated from mid-level sociolinguistic behaviors, including Topic Control, Disagreement and Involvement (Shaikh et al., 2012). In order to calculate effect of the influencer on a group, we track *changes* in the TPN distances between speakers, and particularly between the influencer and other speakers. We want to know if the other speakers in the group moved closer to or further away from the influencer, who may be promoting a particular position on the overall subject of discussion. Our hypothesis is that other participants will move closer (as a group, though not necessarily individually) to an influential speaker. We may also note that some speakers move closer while others move away, indicating a polarizing effect of an influential speaker. If there is more than one influencer in the group these effects may be still more complex.

## 4 Data Collection and Experiment

Our initial focus has been on Twitter discussions which enable users to create messages, i.e., "tweets". There are plenty of tweet messages generated all the time and it is reported that Twitter has surpassed 400 million tweets per day. With the Twitter API, it is easy to collect those tweets for research, as the communications are considered public. However, most of data obtained publicly is of limited value due to its complexity, lack of focus, and inability to control for many independent variables. In order to derive reliable models of conversational behavior that fulfill our interests in opinion change, we needed a controlled environment with participants whose initial opinions were known and with conversation reasonably focused on a topic of interest. To do so, we recruited participants for a two-week Twitter debates on a variety of issues, one of the topics was "Should the minimum legal drinking age be lowered to 18?" We captured participants' initial positions through surveys before each debate, and their exit positions through surveys after the debate was completed two weeks later. The surveys were designed to collect both the participants' opinions about the overall topic of conversation as well as about the roles they played in it. These data were then compared to the automatically computed TPN changes.

### 4.1 Data Collection

To obtain a suitable dataset, we conducted two groups of controlled and secured experiments with Twitter users. The experiment was specially designed to ensure that participants stay on topic of discussion and that there was a minority opinion represented in the group. We assigned the same **overall topic** for both groups: "lowering the drinking age from 21 to 18". Before the discussion, the participants completed an 11-question survey to determine their pre-discussion attitudes toward overall topic. One participant with the minority opinion was then asked to act as an influencer in the discussion, i.e., to try to convince as many people as possible to adopt his or her position. After the discussion, the participants were asked the same 11 questions to determine if their positions have changed. All 11 questions probed various aspects of the overall topic, thus providing a reliable measure of participant's opinion. All responses were on a 7-point scale from "strongly agree" to "strongly disagree". The orientation of individual questions vs. the overall topic was varied to make sure that the participants did not mechanically fill their responses. Some of the questions were:

(1) *Lowering the drinking age to 18 would make alcohol less of a taboo, making alcohol consumption a more normalized activity to be done in moderation.*

+3 strongly agree ----- -3 strongly disagree

(2) *18 year olds are more susceptible to binge drinking and other risky/irresponsible behaviors than people who are 21 and older.*

-3 strongly agree ----- +3 strongly disagree
(note reversed polarity)

The basic statistical information about the two experimental groups is given in Table 1 and the tweet distribution of each participant in Group-1 is shown in Figure 1. Participants are denoted by a two-letter abbreviation (WS, EP and so on). The current data set is only a fraction of a larger corpus, which is currently under development. Additional datasets cover a variety of discussion topics and involve different groups of participants.

| Group | # participants | # tweets | Influencer |
|---|---|---|---|
| 1 | 20 | 225 | WS |
| 2 | 14 | 222 | EP |

Table 1: Selected details of two experimental groups.

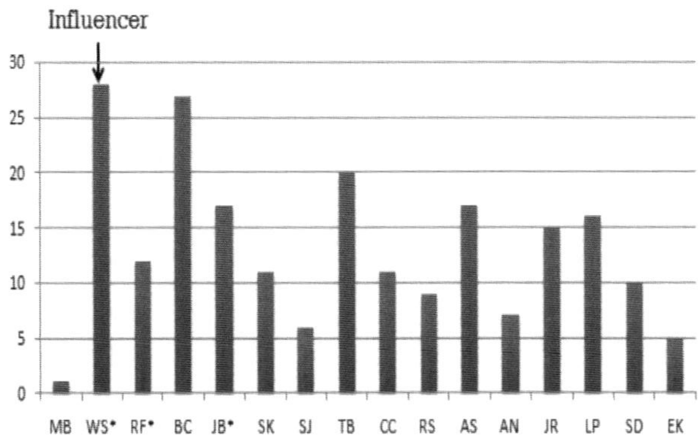


Figure 1: Tweet distribution for each participant in Group-1 where participants with asterisk are against "lowering drinking age".

As we would like to know the participants' pre- and post-discussion attitudes about the overall topic, we used the responses on 11 survey questions to calculate how strongly participants feel on the overall topic of discussion. Each question is given on a seven-point scale ranging from "+3" to "-3", where "+3" implies strongly agree to keep drinking age at 21 and "-3" means strongly disagree. Positions of participants are determined by adding the scores of the 11 questions according to their responses on pre- or post- discussion questionnaires. Figure 2 is an example of pre-discussion responses for two participants in Group-1. WS largely agrees that drinking age should be kept at 21 whereas EK has an opposing opinion. The pre- and post-discussion attitudes of participants in Group-1 towards the overall topic are shown in Figure 3.

| | Q1 | Q2 | Q3 | Q4 | Q5 | Q6 | Q7 | Q8 | Q9 | Q10 | Q11 | Sum |
|---|---|---|---|---|---|---|---|---|---|---|---|---|
| WS | 3 | 0 | 2 | -2 | 0 | -1 | 3 | 3 | 3 | 0 | 0 | 11 |
| EK | -2 | -2 | 1 | 2 | 0 | -2 | -3 | 0 | 0 | -3 | -3 | -12 |

Figure 2: Pre-discussion survey scores of WS and EK.

Subsequently, we computed relative *pre-discussion attitude distance* between each participant and the influencer based on the pre-discussion surveys and their *post-discussion attitude distance* based on the post-discussion surveys. We normalized these distances to a [0, 2] interval to be consistent with cosine distance computation scale used in the TPN module. The changes from pre-discussion attitude distance to post-discussion attitude distance based on the surveys are considered the gold standard against which the system-computed TPN values are measured. As shown in Figure 4(a), the pre-discussion distance between WS and EK is 1.43 (first bar) and the post-discussion distance is 0.07 (second bar), which implies their positions on the overall topic moved significantly closer. We also note that WS's position did not change much throughout the discussion (Figure 3). This was just as we expected since WS was our designated influencer, and this fact was additionally confirmed in the post survey: in response to the question "Who was the influencer in the discussion?" the majority of participants selected WS. The post survey responses from the other group also confirmed our selected influencer. In addition, we used the automated DSARMD system (Strzalkowski et al., 2013) to compute the most influential participants in each group, and again the same people were identified.

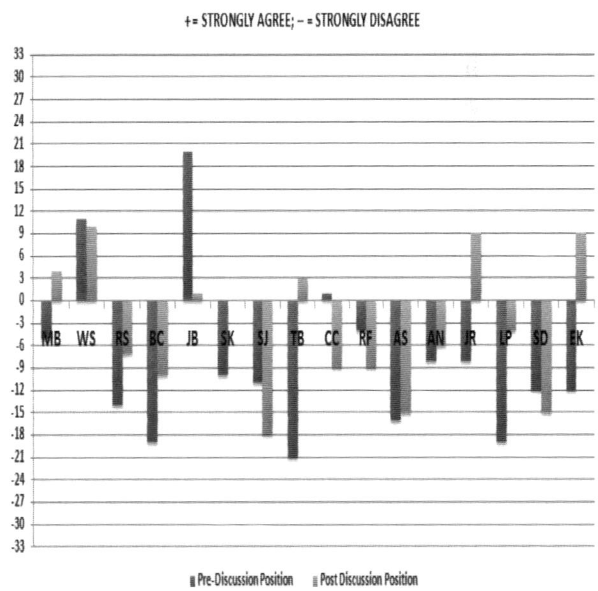


Figure 3: Pre- and post-discussion attitudes of participants in Group-1 where the left bar of the participant is their pre-discussion attitude and right bar of the participant is their post-discussion attitude.

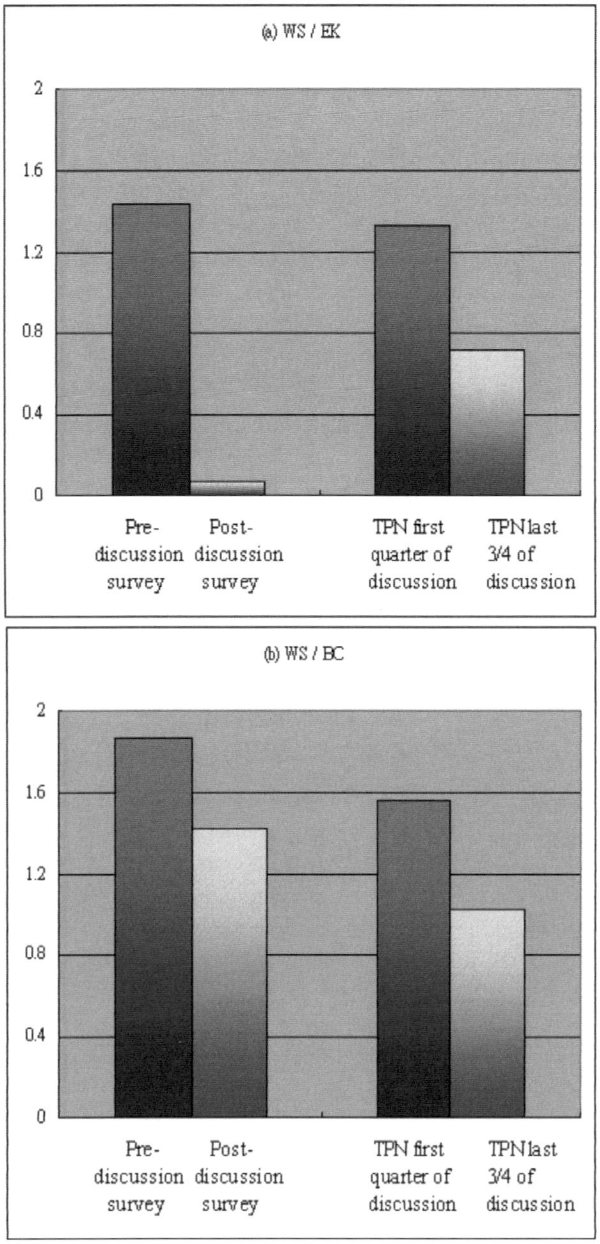


Figure 4: (a) Relative position change between speakers WS (the influencer) and EK based on surveys and automatically computed TPN distance. The first bar in each par corresponds to their pre-discussion distance and second bar is post-discussion distance. We note that TPN predicts correctly that WS and EK move closer together. (b) Relative position change between participants WS and BC.

## 4.2 Experiment

After detailed analysis of participants' opinion before and after the discussion, two twitter discussions are run through our system to extract the required information in order to compute topical positioning as explained in section 3. In Group-1, ten meso-topics were generated by our system (including, e.g., "*drinking age*", "*teens*" and "*alcohol*"). Each participant's polarity associated with these meso-topics was computed by our system to form ten-dimensional topical positioning vectors for Group-1. In our experiment, we used the first quarter of discussion to compute initial topical positioning of the group and last-three quarters to compute the final topical positioning. Once the pre- and post-topical positioning were determined, the topical positioning map between participants was calculated accordingly, i.e., pre- and post-TPN. We used the first quarter of discussion for the initial TPN because we required a sufficient amount of data to compute a stable measure; however, we expected it would not fully represent participants' initial positions. Nonetheless, we should still see the change when compared with post-TPN, which was computed on the last three-quarters of the discussion. In order to detect the opinion shifts and also to measure the effect of the influencer on a group, we tracked the changes in the TPN with respect to the influencer. As shown in Figure 4(a), the pre-TPN between WS and EK is 1.33 (third bar) and post-TPN is 0.72 (fourth bar). Hence, the system determines that their opinions are moving closer which conforms to the survey results. Figure 4(b) is another example of WS and BC that system result shows the same tendency as the survey result. The pre-discussion distance between WS and BC is 1.87 (first bar) and the post-discussion distance is 1.42 (second bar), which implies their positions on the overall topic moved closer after discussion. In system detection, the pre-TPN between is 1.56 (third bar) and post-TPN is 1.02 (fourth bar), which also concludes their attitudes are closer. Another examples showing that speaker moved away from influencer are in Figure 5(a) and 5(b). According to the survey, the pre-discussion attitude distance between WS and CC is 0.62 (first bar) and post-discussion attitude distance is 1.35 (second bar), which implies their positions diverged after the discussion. Our system determined pre-TPN between WS and CC is 1.0 (third bar) and post-

TPN is 1.29 (fourth bar), which shows their divergence.

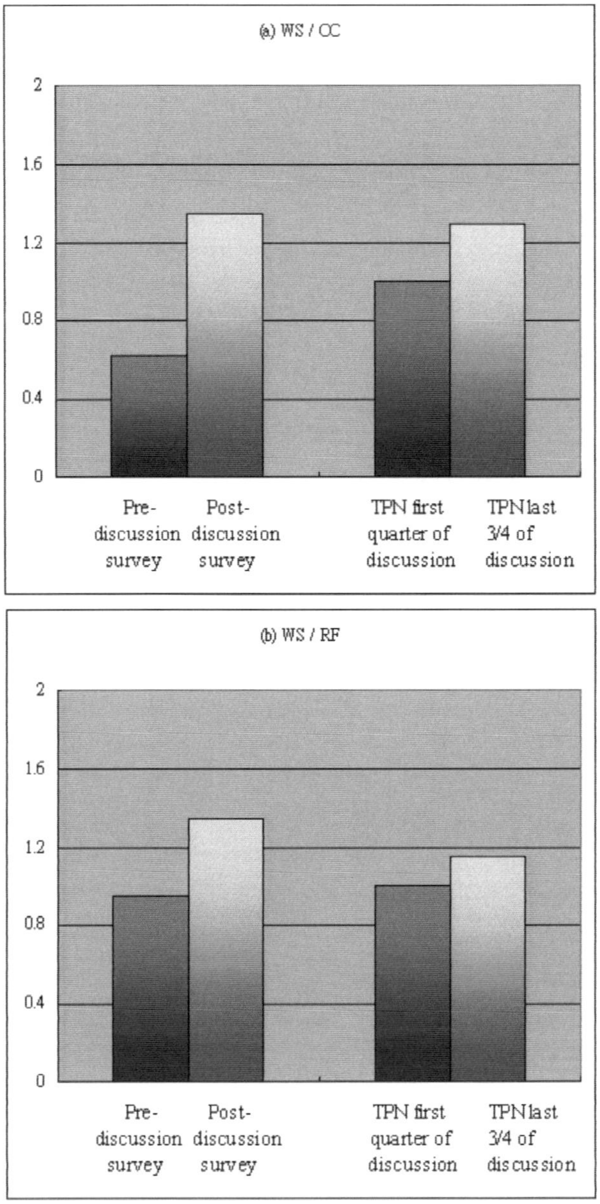


Figure 5: (a) Relative position change between WS and CC based on surveys and TPN. (b) Relative position change between participants WS and RF. We note that RF moves away from WS, which is correctly predicted by TPN.

In a separate exercise we also explored different parts of the Twitter session to compute pre-TPN and post-TPN, in addition to the ¼ vs. ¾ split discussed above. In particular, we computed TPN distances between speakers at first ½ vs. second ½, first ¼ vs. last ¼, first ⅓ vs. last ⅓, etc. Experiment results show that using the first quarter of discussion as initial topical positioning and last quarter as final topical positioning (¼ vs. ¼) produces the most accurate prediction of opinion changes for all group participants: 87.5% in Group-1 and 76% in Group-2. We should also note here that there is no specific correlation between the meso-topics and the overall topic other than the meso-topics arise spontaneously in the conversation. The set of meso-topics in the second discussion on the same topic was different than the in the first discussion. In particular, meso-topics are not necessarily correlated with the aspects of the overall topic that are addressed in the surveys. Nonetheless, the TPN changes appear to predict the changes in surveys in both discussions. At this time the results is indicative only. Further experiments need to be run on additional data (currently being collected) to confirm this finding.

## 5 Conclusion

In this paper, we described an automated approach to detect participant's Topical Positioning and capture the opinion shifts by Topical Position Maps. This work is still in progress and we intend to process more genres of data, including Twitter and online chat, to confirm effects seen in the data we currently have. The future work should be able to account for the relationship between meso-topic and overall topic (i.e., supporting meso-topic means for or against overall topic). A potential solution could be determined by aligning with TPN of influencers who are known strongly pro- or against- overall topic. Another avenue of future work is to apply proposed model on virtual chatroom agent to guide the discussion and change participants' attitudes.

## References

Bradley, M. M., & Lang, P. J. 1999. *Affective norms for English words (ANEW): Instruction manual and affective ratings*(Tech. Rep. No. C-1). Gainesville, FL: University of Florida, The Center for Research in Psychophysiology.

Broadwell, George, Jennifer Stromer-Galley, Tomek Strzalkowski, Samira Shaikh, Sarah Taylor, Umit Boz, Alana Elia, Laura Jiao, Ting Liu, and Nick Webb. "Modeling Socio-Cultural Phenomena in Discourse." *Journal of Natural Language Engineering (2012)*: 1-45.

David, S., and Pinch, T. J. 2006. Six degrees of reputation: The use and abuse of online review and recommendation systems. *First Monday*. Special Issue on Commercial Applications of the Internet.

Fellbaum, C., B. Haskell, H. Langone, G. Miller, R. Poddar, R. Tengi and P. Wakefield. 2006. *WordNet 2.1*.

Hu, M., and Liu, B. 2004. Mining opinion features in customer reviews. *In Proceedings of AAAI*, 755–760.

Klein, D., & Manning, C. D. 2003. Accurate unlexicalized parsing. *In Proceedings of the 41st Annual Meeting on Association for Computational Linguistics-Volume 1* , 423-430. Association for Computational Linguistics.

Martineau, J., & Finin, T. 2009. Delta tfidf: An improved feature space for sentiment analysis. *In Proceedings of the 3rd AAAI International Conference on Weblogs and Social Media*, 258-261.

Philip Beineke, Trevor Hastie, Christopher Manning and Shivakumar Vaithyanathan 2003. An exploration of sentiment summarization. *In Proceedings of AAAI*, 12-15.

Shaikh, Samira, et al 2012. Modeling Influence in Online Multi-party Discourse. *Cloud and Green Computing (CGC), 2012 Second International Conference on. IEEE.*

Small, S., Strzalkowski, T. and Webb, N. 2010. *ECO: Effective Communication Online*. Technical Report ILS-015, University at Albany, SUNY

Somasundaran, S., & Wiebe, J. 2009. Recognizing stances in online debates. *In Proceedings of the Joint Conference of the 47th Annual Meeting of the ACL and the 4th International Joint Conference on Natural Language Processing of the AFNLP.*

Strapparava, C., and Mihalcea, R. 2008. Learning to Identify Emotions in Text. *In Proceedings of the ACM Conference on Applied Computing ACM-SAC.*

Strzalkowski, T.; Broadwell, G. A.; Stromer-Galley, J.; Shaikh, S.; Taylor, S.; and Webb, N. 2010. Modeling socio-cultural phenomena in discourse. *In Proceedings of the 23rd International Conference on Computational Linguistics*, 1038-1046.

Strzalkowski, T., Samira Shaikh, Ting Liu, George Aaron Broadwell, Jennifer Stromer-Galley, Sarah M. Taylor, Veena Ravishankar, Umit Boz, Xiaoai Ren: Influence and Power in Group Interactions. *SBP 2013*: 19-27

Vogt, T., Andre´, E., & Bee, N. 2008. EmoVoice—A framework for online recognition of emotions from voice. *Perception in Multimodal Dialogue Systems*, 188-199.

Wiebe, J., Wilson, T., and Cardie, C. 2005. Annotating expressions of opinions and emotions in language. *Journal of Language Resources and Evaluation 39(2-3)*:165–210

Zhuang, L., Jing, F., Zhu, X. Y., & Zhang, L. 2006. Movie review mining and summarization. *In Conference on Information and Knowledge Management: Proceedings of the 15 th ACM international conference on Information and knowledge management*, 43-50.

# Sentiment Analysis of Political Tweets: Towards an Accurate Classifier

**Akshat Bakliwal**[1], **Jennifer Foster**[2], **Jennifer van der Puil**[3*],
**Ron O'Brien**[4], **Lamia Tounsi**[2] and **Mark Hughes**[5]
[1]Search and Information Extraction Lab, IIIT-Hyderabad, India
[2]NCLT/CNGL, School of Computing, Dublin City University, Ireland
[3]Department of Computer Science and Statistics, Trinity College, Ireland
[4]Quiddity, Dublin, Ireland
[5]CLARITY, School of Computing, Dublin City University, Ireland
[1]akshat.bakliwal@research.iiit.ac.in
[2,5]{jfoster,ltounsi,mhughes}@computing.dcu.ie
[3]jvanderp@tcd.ie
[4]ron@quiddity.ie

## Abstract

We perform a series of 3-class sentiment classification experiments on a set of 2,624 tweets produced during the run-up to the Irish General Elections in February 2011. Even though tweets that have been labelled as sarcastic have been omitted from this set, it still represents a difficult test set and the highest accuracy we achieve is 61.6% using supervised learning and a feature set consisting of subjectivity-lexicon-based scores, Twitter-specific features and the top 1,000 most discriminative words. This is superior to various naive unsupervised approaches which use subjectivity lexicons to compute an overall sentiment score for a <tweet,political_party> pair.

## 1 Introduction

Supervised machine learning using minimal feature engineering has been shown to work well in binary positive/negative sentiment classification tasks on well-behaved datasets such as movie reviews (Pang et al., 2002). In this paper we describe sentiment analysis experiments in a more complicated setup: the task is three-class positive/negative/neutral classification, the sentiment being classified is not at the general document level but rather directed towards a topic, the documents are tweets, and the topic is politics, specifically the Irish General Election of February 2011.

The dataset used in the experiments contains tweets which were collected in the run up to the election and which were subsequently doubly annotated as positive, negative or neutral towards a particular political party or party leader. The annotators also marked a tweet as sarcastic if its literal sentiment was different to its actual sentiment. Before exploring the thorny issue of sentiment classification in the face of sarcasm, we simplify the problem by first trying to establish some sentiment analysis baselines for those tweets which were not deemed to be sarcastic.

We first explore a naive approach in which a subjectivity lexicon is used as the primary source of information in determining whether sentiment towards a political party or party leader is positive, negative or neutral. The best version of this method achieves an accuracy of 58.9, an absolute improvement of 4.9 points over the majority baseline (54%) in which all tweets are classified as neutral. When these lexicon scores are combined with bag-of-word features and some Twitter-specific features in a supervised machine learning setup, this accuracy increases to 61.6%.

The paper is organised as follows: related work is described in Section 2, followed by a brief discussion of the 2011 Irish General Election in Section 3, a description of the dataset in Section 4 and a description of the natural language processing tools and resources employed in Section 5. In Section 6, the unsupervised lexicon-based approach is presented and its limitations discussed. Section 7 describes the machine-learning-based experiments and Section 8 concludes and provides hints towards fu-

*Akshat Bakliwal and Jennifer van der Puil carried out their part of this work while employed as summer interns at the Centre for Next Generation Localisation(CNGL) in the School of Computing, DCU.

ture work with this new dataset.

## 2 Previous Work

The related work can be divided into two groups, general sentiment analysis research and research which is devoted specifically to the political domain.

### 2.1 General Sentiment Analysis

Research in the area of sentiment mining started with product (Turney, 2002) and movie (Pang et al., 2002) reviews. Turney (2002) used Pointwise Mutual Information (PMI) to estimate the sentiment orientation of phrases. Pang et al. (2002) employed supervised learning with various set of n-gram features, achieving an accuracy of almost 83% with unigram presence features on the task of document-level binary sentiment classification. Research on other domains and genres including blogs (Chesley, 2006) and news (Godbole et al., 2007) followed.

Early sentiment analysis research focused on longer documents such as movie reviews and blogs. Microtext on the other hand restricts the writer to a more concise expression of opinion. Smeaton and Bermingham (2010) tested the hypothesis that it is easier to classify sentiment in microtext as compared to longer documents. They experimented with microtext from Twitter, microreviews from *blippr*, blog posts and movie reviews and concluded that it is easier to identify sentiment from microtext. However, as they move from contextually sparse unigrams to higher n-grams, it becomes more difficult to improve the performance of microtext sentiment classification, whereas higher-order information makes it easier to perform classification of longer documents.

There has been some research on the use of positive and negative emoticons and hashtags in tweets as a proxy for sentiment labels (Go et al., 2009; Pak and Paroubek, 2010; Davidov et al., 2010; Bora, 2012). Bakliwal et al. (2012) emphasized the importance of preprocessing and proposed a set of features to extract maximum sentiment information from tweets. They used unigram and bigram features along with features which are more associated with tweets such as emoticons, hashtags, URLs, etc. and showed that combining linguistic and Twitter-specific features can boost the classification accuracy.

### 2.2 Political Sentiment Analysis

In recent years, there has been growing interest in mining online political sentiment in order to predict the outcome of elections. One of the most influential papers is that of Tumasjan et al. (2010) who focused on the 2009 German federal election and investigated whether Twitter can be used to predict election outcomes. Over one hundred thousand tweets dating from August 13 to September 19, 2009 containing the names of the six parties represented in the German parliament were collected. LIWC 2007 (Pennebaker et al., 2007) was then used to extract sentiment from the tweets. LIWC is a text analysis software developed to assess emotional, cognitive and structural components of text samples using a psychometrically validated internal dictionary. Tumasjan et al. concluded that the number of tweets/mentions of a party is directly proportional to the probability of winning the elections.

O'Connor et al. (2010) investigated the extent to which public opinion polls were correlated with political sentiment expressed in tweets. Using the Subjectivity Lexicon (Wilson et al., 2005), they estimate the daily sentiment scores for each entity. A tweet is defined as positive if it contains a positive word and vice versa. A sentiment score for that day is calculated as the ratio of the positive count over the negative count. They find that their sentiment scores were correlated with opinion polls on presidential job approval but less strongly with polls on electoral outcome.

Choy et al. (2011) discuss the application of online sentiment detection to predict the vote percentage for each of the candidates in the Singapore presidential election of 2011. They devise a formula to calculate the percentage vote each candidate will receive using census information on variables such as age group, sex, location, etc. They combine this with a sentiment-lexicon-based sentiment analysis engine which calculates the sentiment in each tweet and aggregates the positive and negative sentiment for each candidate. Their model was able to predict the narrow margin between the top two candidates but failed to predict the correct winner.

Wang et al. (2012) proposed a real-time sentiment analysis system for political tweets which was based on the U.S. presidential election of 2012. They collected over 36 million tweets and collected the sentiment annotations using Amazon Mechanical Turk. Using a Naive Bayes model with unigram features, their system achieved 59% accuracy on the four-category classification.

Bermingham and Smeaton (2011) are also concerned with predicting electoral outcome, in particular, the outcome of the Irish General Election of 2011 (the same election that we focused on). They analyse political sentiment in tweets by means of supervised classification with unigram features and an annotated dataset different to and larger than the one we present, achieving 65% accuracy on the task of *positive/negative/neutral* classification. They conclude that volume is a stronger indicator of election outcome than sentiment, but that sentiment still has a role to play.

Gayo-Avello (2012) calls into question the use of Twitter for election outcome prediction. Previous works which report positive results on this task using data from Twitter are surveyed and shortcomings in their methodology and/or assumptions noted. In this paper, our focus is not the (non-) predictive nature of political tweets but rather the accurate identification of any sentiment expressed in the tweets. If the accuracy of sentiment analysis of political tweets can be improved (or its limitations at least better understood) then this will likely have a positive effect on its usefulness as an alternative or complement to traditional opinion polling.

## 3 #ge11: The Irish General Election 2011

The Irish general elections were held on February 25, 2011. 165 representatives were elected across 43 constituencies for the Dáil, the main house of parliament. Eight parties nominated their candidates for election and a coalition (Fine Gael and Labour) government was formed. The parties in the outgoing coalition government, Fianna Fáil and the Greens, suffered disastrous defeats, the worst defeat of a sitting government since the foundatation of the State in 1922.

Gallagher and Marsh (2011, chapter 5) discuss the use of social media by parties, candidates and voters in the 2011 election and conclude that it had a much more important role to play in this election than in the previous one in 2007. On the role of Twitter in particular, they report that *"Twitter was less widespread among candidates [than Facebook], but it offered the most diverse source of citizen coverage during the election, and it has been integrated into several mainstream media"*. They estimated that 7% of the Irish population had a Twitter account at the time of the election.

## 4 Dataset

We compiled a corpus of tweets using the Twitter search API between 20th and the 25th of January 2011 (one month before the election). We selected the main political entities (the five biggest political parties – Fianna Fáil, Fine Gael, Labour, Sinn Féin and the Greens – and their leaders) and perform query-based search to collect the tweets relating to these entities. The resulting dataset contains 7,916 tweets of which 4,710 are retweets or duplicates, leaving a total of 3,206 tweets.

The tweets were annotated by two Irish annotators with a knowledge of the Irish political landscape. Disagreements between the two annotators were studied and resolved by a third annotator. The annotators were asked to identify the sentiment associated with the topic (or entity) of the tweet. Annotation was performed using the following 6 labels:

- **pos**: Tweets which carry positive sentiment towards the topic
- **neg**: Tweets which carry negative sentiment towards the topic
- **mix**: Tweets which carry both positive and negative sentiment towards the topic
- **neu**: Tweets which do not carry any sentiment towards the topic
- **nen**: Tweets which were written in languages other than English.
- **non**: Tweets which do not have any mention or relation to the topic. These represent search errors.

In addition to the above six classes, annotators were asked to flag whether a tweet was sarcastic.

The dataset which we use for the experiments described in this paper contains only those tweets

| | | |
|---|---|---|
| **Positive Tweets** | 256 | 9.75% |
| **Negative Tweets** | 950 | 36.22% |
| **Neutral Tweets** | 1418 | 54.03% |
| **Total Tweets** | 2624 | |

Table 1: Class Distribution

that have been labelled as either positive, negative or neutral, i.e. non-relevant, mixed-sentiment and non-English tweets are discarded. We also simplify our task by omitting those tweets which have been flagged as sarcastic by one or both of the annotators, leaving a set of 2,624 tweets with a class distribution as shown in Table 1.

## 5 Tools and Resources

In the course of our experiments, we use two different subjectivity lexicons, one part-of-speech tagger and one parser. For part-of-speech tagging we use a tagger (Gimpel et al., 2011) designed specifically for tweets. For parsing, we use the Stanford parser (Klein and Manning, 2003). To identify the sentiment polarity of a word we use:

1. **Subjectivity Lexicon (SL)** (Wilson et al., 2005): This lexicon contains 8,221 words (6,878 unique forms) of which 3,249 are adjectives, 330 are adverbs, 1,325 are verbs, 2,170 are nouns and remaining (1,147) words are marked as *anypos*. There are many words which occur with two or more different part-of-speech tags. We extend SL with 341 domain-specific words to produce an extended SL.

2. **SentiWordNet 3.0 (SWN)** (Baccianella et al., 2010): With over 100+ thousand words, SWN is far larger than SL but is likely to be noisier since it has been built semi-automatically. Each word in the lexicon is associated with both a positive and negative score, and an objective score given by (1), i.e. the positive, negative and objective score sum to 1.

$$ObjScore = 1 - PosScore - NegScore \quad (1)$$

## 6 Naive Lexicon-based Classification

In this section we describe a naive approach to sentiment classification which does not make use of labelled training data but rather uses the information in a sentiment lexicon to deduce the sentiment orientation towards a political party in a tweet (see Liu (2010) for an overview of this unsupervised lexicon-based approach). In Section 6.1, we present the basic method along with some variants which improve on the basic method by making use of information about part-of-speech, negation and distance from the topic. In Section 6.2, we examine some of the cases which remain misclassified by our best lexicon-based method. In Section 6.3, we discuss briefly those tweets that have been labelled as sarcastic.

### 6.1 Method and Results

Our baseline lexicon-based approach is as follows: we look up each word in our sentiment lexicon and sum up the scores to corresponding scalars. The results are shown in Table 2. Note that the most likely estimated class prediction is neutral with a probability of .5403 (1418/2624).

#### 6.1.1 Which Subjectivity Lexicon?

The first column shows the results that we obtain when the lexicon we use is our extended version of the SL lexicon. The results in the second column are those that result from using SWN. In the third column, we combine the two lexicons. We define a combination pattern of Extended-SL and SWN in which we prioritize Extended-SL because it is manually checked and some domain-specific words are added. For the words which were missing from Extended-SL (SWN), we assign them the polarity of SWN (Extended-SL). Table 3 explains exactly how the scores from the two lexicons are combined. Although SWN slightly outperforms Extended-SL for the baseline lexicon-based approach (first row of Table 2), it is outperformed by Extended-SL and the combinaton of the two lexicons for all the variants. We can conclude from the full set of results in Table 2 that SWN is less useful than Extended-SL or the combination of SWN and Extended-SL.

#### 6.1.2 Filtering by Part-of-Speech

The results in the first row of Table 2 represent our baseline experiment in which each word in the tweet is looked up in the sentiment lexicon and its sentiment score added to a running total. We achieve a classification accuracy of 52.44% with the

| Method | Extended-SL | | SWN | | Combined | |
|---|---|---|---|---|---|---|
| 3-Class Classification (Pos vs Neg vs Neu) | Correct | Accuracy | Correct | Accuracy | Correct | Accuracy |
| Baseline | 1376 | 52.44% | 1379 | 52.55% | 1288 | 49.09% |
| Baseline + Adj | 1457 | 55.53% | 1449 | 55.22% | 1445 | 55.07% |
| Baseline + Adj + S | 1480 | 56.40% | 1459 | 55.60% | 1481 | 56.44% |
| Baseline + Adj + S + Neg | 1495 | 56.97% | 1462 | 55.72% | 1496 | 57.01% |
| Baseline + Adj + S + Neg + Phrases | 1511 | 57.58% | 1479 | 56.36% | 1509 | 57.51% |
| Baseline + Adj + S + Neg + Phrases + Than | 1533 | 58.42% | 1502 | 57.24% | 1533 | 58.42% |
| Distance Based Scoring: Baseline + Adj + S + Neg + Phrases + Than | 1545 | 58.88% | 1506 | 57.39% | 1547 | **58.96%** |
| Sarcastic Tweets | 87/344 | 25.29% | 81/344 | 23.55% | 87/344 | 25.29% |

Table 2: 3-class classification using the naive lexicon-based approach. The majority baseline is 54.03%.

| Extended-SL polarity | SWN Polarity | Combination Polarity |
|---|---|---|
| -1 | -1 | -2 |
| -1 | 0 | -1 |
| -1 | 1 | -1 |
| 0 | -1 | -0.5 |
| 0 | 0 | 0 |
| 0 | 1 | 0.5 |
| 1 | -1 | 1 |
| 1 | 0 | 1 |
| 1 | 1 | 2 |

Table 3: Combination Scheme of extended-SL and SWN. Here 0 represents either a neutral word or a word missing from the lexicon.

Extended-SL lexicon. We speculate that this low accuracy is occurring because too many words that appear in the sentiment lexicon are included in the overall sentiment score without actually contributing to the sentiment towards the topic. To refine our approach one step further, we use part-of-speech information and consider only adjectives for the classification of tweets since adjectives are strong indicators of sentiment (Hatzivassiloglou and Wiebe, 2000). We achieve an accuracy improvement of approximately three absolute points, and this improvement holds true for both sentiment lexicons. This supports our hypothesis that we are using irrelevant information for classification in the baseline system.

Our next improvement (third row of Table 2) comes from mapping all inflected forms to their stems (using the Porter stemmer). Examples of inflected forms that are reduced to their stems are *delighted* or *delightful*. Using stemming with adjectives over the baseline, we achieve an accuracy of 56.40% with Extended-SL.

#### 6.1.3 Negation

*"Negation is a very common linguistic construction that affects polarity and, therefore, needs to be taken into consideration in sentiment analysis"* (Councill et al., 2010). We perform negation handling in tweets using two different approaches. In the first approach, we first identify negation words

and reverse the polarity of sentiment-bearing words within a window of three words. In the second approach, we try to resolve the scope of the negation using syntactic parsing. The Stanford dependency scheme (de Marneffe and Manning, 2008) has a special relation (`neg`) to indicate negation. We reverse the sentiment polarity of a word marked via the `neg` relation as being in the scope of a negation. Using the first approach, we see an improvement of 0.6% in the classification accuracy with the Extended-SL lexicon. Using the second approach, we see an improvement of 0.5%. Since there appears to be very little difference between the two approaches to negation-handling and in order to reduce the computational burden of running the Stanford parser each time to obtain the dependencies, we continue further experiments with the first method only. Using baseline + stemming + adjectives + neg we achieve an accuracy of 56.97% with the Extended-SL lexicon.

#### 6.1.4 Domain-specific idioms

In the context of political tweets we see many sentiment-bearing idioms and fixed expressions, e.g. *god save us*, *X for Taoiseach*[1], *wolf in sheep's clothing*, etc. In our study, we had a total of 89 phrases. When we directly account for these phrases, we achieve an accuracy of 57.58% (an absolute improvement of 0.6 points over the last step).

#### 6.1.5 Comparative Expressions

Another form of expressing an opinion towards an entity is by comparing the entity with some other entity. For example consider the tweet:

*Fast Food sounds like a better vote than Fianna Fail.* (2)

In this tweet, an indirect negative sentiment is expressed towards the political party *Fianna Fáil*. In order to take into account such constructions, the following procedure is applied: we divide the tweet into two parts, left and right. The left part contains the text which comes before the *than* and the right part contains the text which comes after *than*, e.g.
**Tweet**: 'X is better than Y'
**Left**: 'X is better'
**Right**: 'Y'.

[1] The term *Taoiseach* refers to the Irish Prime Minister.

We then use the following strategy to calculate the polarity of the tweet oriented towards the entity:

$$\begin{aligned}
S_left &= sentiment\ score\ of\ Left.\\
S_right &= sentiment\ score\ of\ Right.\\
Ent_pos_left &= if\ entity\ is\ left\ of\\
&\quad `than',\ then\ 1,\ otherwise\ -1.\\
Ent_pos_right &= if\ entity\ is\ right\ of\\
&\quad `than',\ then\ 1,\ otherwise\ -1.\\
S(tweet) &= Ent_pos_left * S_left +\\
&\quad Ent_pos_right * S_right. \qquad (3)
\end{aligned}$$

So in (2) above the entity, *Fianna Fáil*, is to the right of *than* meaning that its *Ent_pos_right* value is 1 and its *Ent_pos_left* value is -1. This has the effect of flipping the polarity of the positive word *better*. By including the "than" comparison, we see an improvement of absolute 0.8% (third last row of Table 2).

#### 6.1.6 Distance Scoring

To emphasize the topic-oriented nature of our sentiment classification, we also define a distance-based scoring function where we define the overall score of the tweet as given in (4). Here $dis(word)$ is defined as number of words between the topic (i.e. the political entity) and the sentiment word.

$$S(tweet) = \sum_{i=1}^{n} S(word_i)/dis(word_i). \qquad (4)$$

The addition of the distance information further enhanced our system accuracy by 0.45%, taking it to 58.88% (second last row of Table 2). Our highest overall accuracy (58.96) is achieved in this setting using the combined lexicon.

It should be noted that this lexicon-based approach is overfitting to our dataset since the list of domain-specific phrases and the form of the comparative constructions have been obtained from the dataset itself. This means that we are making a strong assumption about the representativeness of this dataset and accuracy on a held-out test set is likely to be lower.

### 6.2 Error Analysis

In this section we discuss pitfalls of the naive lexicon-based approach with the help of some examples (see Table 4). Consider the first example from the table, *@username and u believe people in fianna fail . What are you a numbskull or a journalist ?* In this tweet, we see that negative sentiment is imparted by the question part of the tweet, but actually there are no sentiment adjectives. The word *numbskull* is contributing to the sentiment but is tagged as a noun and not as an adjective. This tweet is tagged as negative by our annotators and as neutral by our lexicon-based classifier.

Consider the second example from Table 4, *@username LOL . A guy called to our house tonight selling GAA tickets . His first words were : I'm not from Fianna Fail .* This is misclassified because there are no sentiment bearing words according to the sentiment lexicon. The last tweet in the table represents another example of the same problem. Note however that the emoticon :/ in the last tweet and the web acronym LOL in the second tweet are providing hints which our system is not making use of.

In the third example from Table 4, *@username Such scary words .' Sinn Fein could top the poll ' in certain constituencies . I feel sick at the thought of it . '* In this example, we have three sentiment bearing words: *scary*, *top* and *sick*. Two of the three words are negative and one word is positive. The word *scary* is stemmed incorrectly as *scari* which means that it is out of the scope of our lexicons. If we just count the number of sentiment words remaining, then this tweet is labelled as neutral but actually is negative with respect to the party *Sinn Féin*. We proposed the use of distance as a measure of relatedness to the topic and we observed a minor improvement in classification accuracy. However, for this example, the distance-based approach does not work. The word *top* is just two words away from the topic and thus contributes the maximum, resulting in the whole tweet being misclassified as positive.

### 6.3 Sarcastic Tweets

"*Political discouse is plagued with humor, double entendres, and sarcasm; this makes determining political preference of users hard and inferring voting intention even harder.*"(Gayo-Avello, 2012)

As part of the annotation process, annotators were asked to indicate whether they thought a tweet exhibited sarcasm. Some examples of tweets that were annotated as sarcastic are shown in Table 5.

We made the decision to omit these tweets from the main sentiment classification experiments under the assumption that they constituted a special case which would be better handled by a different classifier. This decision is vindicated by the results in the last row of Table 2 which show what happens when we apply our best classifier (*Distance-based Scoring: Baseline+Adj+S+Neg+Phrases+Than*) to the sarcastic tweets – only a quarter of them are correctly classified. Even with a very large and highly domain-tuned lexicon, the lexicon-based approach on its own will struggle to be of use for cases such as these, but the situation might be improved were the lexicon to be used in conjunction with possible sarcasm indicators such as exclamation marks.

## 7 Supervised Machine Learning

Although our dataset is small, we investigate whether we can improve over the lexicon-based approach by using supervised machine learning. As our learning algorithm, we employ support vector machines in a 5-fold cross validation setup. The tool we use is SVMLight (Joachims, 1999).

We explore two sets of features. The first are the tried-and-tested unigram presence features which have been used extensively not only in sentiment analysis but in other text classification tasks. As we have only 2,624 training samples, we performed feature selection by ranking the features using the Chi-squared metric.

The second feature set consists of 25 features which are inspired by the work on lexicon-based classification described in the previous section. These are the counts of positive, negative, objective words according to each of the three lexicons and the corresponding sentiment scores for the overall tweets. In total there are 19 such features. We also employ six Twitter-related presence features: positive emoticons, negative emoticons, URLs, positive hashtags, negative hashtags and neutral hashtags. For further reference we call this second set of features our "hand-crafted" features.

The results are shown in Table 6. We can see that using the hand-crafted features alone barely improves over the majority baseline of 54.03 but it does improve over our baseline lexicon-based approach (see first row of Table 2). Encouragingly, we see some benefit from using these features in conjunc-

| Tweet | Topic | Manual Polarity | Calculated Polarity | Reason for misclassification |
|---|---|---|---|---|
| *@username and u believe people in fianna fail . What are you a numbskull or a journalist ?* | Fianna Fáil | neg | neu | Focus only on adjectives |
| *@username LOL . A guy called to our house tonight selling GAA tickets . His first words were : I'm not from Fianna Fail .* | Fianna Fáil | neg | neu | No sentiment words |
| *@username Such scary words .' Sinn Fein could top the poll ' in certain constituencies . I feel sick at the thought of it .* | Sinn Féin | neg | pos | Stemming and word distance order |
| *@username more RTE censorship . Why are they so afraid to let Sinn Fein put their position across . Certainly couldn't be worse than ff* | Sinn Féin | pos | neg | contribution of *afraid* |
| *Based on this programme the winners will be Sinn Fein & Gilmore for not being there #rtefl* | Sinn Féin | pos | neu | Focus only on adjectives |
| *#thefrontline pearce Doherty is a spoofer ! Vote sinn fein and we loose more jobs* | Sinn Féin | neg | pos | Focus only on adjectives & contribution of phrase *Vote X* |
| *@username Tread carefully Conor . BNP endorsing Sinn Fin etc . etc .* | Sinn Féin | neg | neu | No sentiment words |
| *@username ah dude . You made me go to the fine gael web site ! :/* | Fine Gael | neg | neu | No sentiment words |

Table 4: Misclassification Examples

| Feature Set | # Features | Accuracy |
|---|---|---|
| # samples = 2624 | | SVM Light |
| Hand-crafted | 25 | 54.76 |
| Unigram | 7418 | 55.22 |
| | Top 1000 | 58.92 |
| | Top 100 | 56.86 |
| Unigram + Hand-crafted | 7444 | 54.73 |
| | Top 1000 | **61.62** |
| | Top 100 | 59.53 |

Table 6: Results of 3-Class Classification using Supervised Machine Learning

tion with the unigram features. Our best overall result of 61.62% is achieved by using the Top 1000 unigram features together with these hand-crafted features. This result seems to suggest that, even with only a few thousand training instances, employing supervised machine learning is still worthwhile.

## 8 Conclusion

We have introduced a new dataset of political tweets which will be made available for use by other researchers. Each tweet in this set has been annotated for sentiment towards a political entity, as well as for the presence of sarcasm. Omitting the sarcastic tweets from our experiments, we show that we can classify a tweet as being positive, negative or neutral towards a particular political party or party leader with an accuracy of almost 59% using a simple approach based on lexicon lookup. This improves over the majority baseline by almost 5 absolute percentage points but as the classifier uses information from the test set itself, the result is likely to be lower on a held-out test set. The accuracy increases slightly when the lexicon-based information is encoded as features and employed together with bag-of-word features in a supervised machine learning setup.

Future work involves carrying out further exper-

| Sarcastic Tweets |
| --- |
| *Ah bless Brian Cowen's little cotton socks! He's staying on as leader of FF because its better for the country. How selfless!* |
| *So now Brian Cowen is now Minister for foreign affairs and Taoiseach? Thats exactly what he needs more responsibilities http://bbc.in/hJI0hb* |
| *Mary Harney is going. Surprise surprise! Brian Cowen is going to be extremely busy with all these portfolios to administer. Super hero!* |
| *Now in its darkest hour Fianna Fail needs. . . Ivor!* |
| *Labour and Fine Gael have brought the election forward by 16 days Crisis over Ireland is SAVED!! #vinb* |
| *@username Maybe one of those nice Sinn Fein issue boiler suits? #rtefl* |
| *I WILL vote for Fine Gael if they pledge to dress James O'Reilly as a leprechaun and send him to the White House for Paddy's Day.* |

Table 5: Examples of tweets which have been flagged as sarcastic

iments on those tweets that have been annotated as sarcastic, exploring the use of syntactic dependency paths in the computation of distance between a word and the topic, examining the role of training set class bias on the supervised machine learning results and exploring the use of distant supervision to obtain more training data for this domain.

## Acknowledgements

Thanks to Emmet O Briain, Lesley Ni Bhriain and the anonymous reviewers for their helpful comments. This research has been supported by Enterprise Ireland (CFTD/2007/229) and by Science Foundation Ireland (Grant 07/CE/ I1142) as part of the CNGL (www.cngl.ie) at the School of Computing, DCU.

## References

Stefano Baccianella, Andrea Esuli, and Fabrizio Sebastiani. 2010. Sentiwordnet 3.0: An enhanced lexical resource for sentiment analysis and opinion mining. In *Proceedings of the Seventh International Conference on Language Resources and Evaluation (LREC'10).*

Akshat Bakliwal, Piyush Arora, Senthil Madhappan, Nikhil Kapre, Mukesh Singh, and Vasudeva Varma. 2012. Mining sentiments from tweets. In *Proceedings of the WASSA'12 in conjunction with ACL'12.*

Adam Bermingham and Alan F. Smeaton. 2010. Classifying sentiment in microblogs: is brevity an advantage? In *Proceedings of the 19th ACM international conference on Information and Knowledge Management.*

Adam Bermingham and Alan Smeaton. 2011. On using Twitter to monitor political sentiment and predict election results. In *Proceedings of the Workshop on Sentiment Analysis where AI meets Psychology (SAAIP 2011).*

Nibir Nayan Bora. 2012. Summarizing public opinions in tweets. In *Journal Proceedings of CICLing 2012.*

Paula Chesley. 2006. Using verbs and adjectives to automatically classify blog sentiment. In *Proceedings of AAAI-CAAW-06, the Spring Symposia on Computational Approaches.*

Murphy Choy, Michelle L. F. Cheong, Ma Nang Laik, and Koo Ping Shung. 2011. A sentiment analysis of Singapore Presidential Election 2011 using Twitter data with census correction. *CoRR*, abs/1108.5520.

Isaac G. Councill, Ryan McDonald, and Leonid Velikovich. 2010. What's great and what's not: learning to classify the scope of negation for improved sentiment analysis. In *Proceedings of the Workshop on Negation and Speculation in Natural Language Processing*, NeSp-NLP '10.

Dmitry Davidov, Oren Tsur, and Ari Rappoport. 2010. Enhanced sentiment learning using Twitter hashtags and smileys. In *Proceedings of the 23rd International Conference on Computational Linguistics: Posters.*

Marie-Catherine de Marneffe and Christopher D. Manning. 2008. The stanford typed dependencies representation. In *Proceedings of the COLING Workshop on Cross-Framework and Cross-Domain Parser Evaluation.*

Michael Gallagher and Michael Marsh. 2011. *How Ireland Voted 2011: The Full Story of Ireland's Earthquake Election.* Palgrave Macmillan.

Daniel Gayo-Avello. 2012. "I wanted to predict elections with Twitter and all I got was this lousy paper".

A balanced survey on election prediction using Twitter data. *CoRR*, abs/1204.6441.

Kevin Gimpel, Nathan Schneider, Brendan O'Connor, Dipanjan Das, Daniel Mills, Jacob Eisenstein, Michael Heilman, Dani Yogatama, Jeffrey Flanigan, and Noah A. Smith. 2011. Part-of-speech tagging for Twitter: annotation, features, and experiments. In *Proceedings of the 49th Annual Meeting of the Association for Computational Linguistics: Human Language Technologies: short papers - Volume 2*.

Alec Go, Richa Bhayani, and Lei Huang. 2009. Twitter sentiment classification using distant supervision. In *CS224N Project Report, Stanford University*.

Namrata Godbole, Manjunath Srinivasaiah, and Steven Skiena. 2007. Large-scale sentiment analysis for news and blogs. In *Proceedings of the International Conference on Weblogs and Social Media (ICWSM)*.

Vasileios Hatzivassiloglou and Janyce M. Wiebe. 2000. Effects of adjective orientation and gradability on sentence subjectivity. In *Proceedings of COLING*.

Thorsten Joachims. 1999. Advances in kernel methods. chapter Making large-scale support vector machine learning practical, pages 169–184. MIT Press, Cambridge, MA, USA.

Dan Klein and Christopher D. Manning. 2003. Accurate unlexicalized parsing. In *Proceedings of the 41st Annual Meeting on Association for Computational Linguistics - Volume 1*.

Bing Liu. 2010. Handbook of natural language processing. chapter Sentiment Analysis and Subjectivity. Chapman and Hall.

Brendan O'Connor, Ramnath Balasubramanyan, Bryan R. Routledge, and Noah A. Smith. 2010. From tweets to polls: Linking text sentiment to public opinion time series. In *Proceedings of the International Conference on Weblogs and Social Media (ICWSM)*.

Alexander Pak and Patrick Paroubek. 2010. Twitter as a corpus for sentiment analysis and opinion mining. In *Proceedings of the Seventh International Conference on Language Resources and Evaluation (LREC'10)*.

Bo Pang, Lillian Lee, and Shivakumar Vaithyanathan. 2002. Thumbs up?: sentiment classification using machine learning techniques. In *Proceedings of the conference on Empirical Methods in Natural Language Processing - Volume 10*.

James W. Pennebaker, Cindy K. Chung, Molly Ireland, Amy Gonzales, and Roger J. Booth. 2007. The development and psychometric properties of liwc2007. Technical report, Austin,Texas.

Andranik Tumasjan, Timm Oliver Sprenger, Philipp G. Sandner, and Isabell M. Welpe. 2010. Predicting elections with Twitter: What 140 characters reveal about political sentiment. In *Proceedings of the International Conference on Weblogs and Social Media*.

Peter D. Turney. 2002. Thumbs up or thumbs down?: semantic orientation applied to unsupervised classification of reviews. In *Proceedings of the 40th Annual Meeting on Association for Computational Linguistics*.

Hao Wang, Dogan Can, Abe Kazemzadeh, François Bar, and Shrikanth Narayanan. 2012. A system for real-time Twitter sentiment analysis of 2012 U.S. presidential election cycle. In *ACL (System Demonstrations)*.

Theresa Wilson, Janyce Wiebe, and Paul Hoffmann. 2005. Recognizing contextual polarity in phrase-level sentiment analysis. In *Proceedings of the conference on Human Language Technology and Empirical Methods in Natural Language Processing*.

# A Case Study of Sockpuppet Detection in Wikipedia

**Thamar Solorio** and **Ragib Hasan** and **Mainul Mizan**
The University of Alabama at Birmingham
1300 University Blvd.
Birmingham, AL 35294, USA
{solorio,ragib,mainul}@cis.uab.edu

## Abstract

This paper presents preliminary results of using authorship attribution methods for the detection of sockpuppeteering in Wikipedia. Sockpuppets are fake accounts created by malicious users to bypass Wikipedia's regulations. Our dataset is composed of the comments made by the editors on the talk pages. To overcome the limitations of the short lengths of these comments, we use an voting scheme to combine predictions made on individual user entries. We show that this approach is promising and that it can be a viable alternative to the current human process that Wikipedia uses to resolve suspected sockpuppet cases.

## 1 Introduction

Collaborative projects in social media have become very popular in recent years. A very successful example of this is Wikipedia, which has emerged as the world's largest crowd-sourced encyclopaedia. This type of decentralized collaborative processes are extremely vulnerable to vandalism and malicious behavior. Anyone can edit articles in Wikipedia and/or make comments in article discussion pages. Registration is not mandatory, but anyone can register an account in Wikipedia by providing only little information about themselves. This ease of creating an identity has led malicious users to create multiple identities and use them for various purposes, ranging from block evasion, false majority opinion claims, and vote stacking. This is an example of the multi aliasing problem known as "The Sybil Attack" (Douceur, 2002). Unfortunately, Wikipedia does not provide any facility to detect such multiple identities. The current process is carried out by humans, is very time consuming, and final resolution to cases of multiple identities is based on human intuition. A smart sockpuppet can therefore evade detection by using multiple IP addresses, modifying writing style, and changing behavior. Also, a malicious user can create sleeper accounts that perform benign edits from time to time, but are used for sockpuppetry when needed. Identifying such accounts as sockpuppets is not obvious as these accounts may have a long and diverse edit history.

Sockpuppets are a prevalent problem in Wikipedia, there were close to 2,700 unique suspected cases reported in 2012. In this paper, we present a small scale study of automated detection of sockpuppets based on machine learning. We approach this problem from the point of view of authorship attribution (AA), where the task consists of analyzing a written document to predict the true author. If we can successfully model the editors' unique writing style from their comments, then we can use this information to link the sockpuppet accounts to their corresponding puppeteer. We focus on the content from the talk pages since the articles edited on Wikipedia have a fixed and very uniform style. In contrast, we have observed that editors write in a more free-form style during discussions carried out on the talk pages. Our results show that a two-stage process for the task can achieve promising results.

The contributions of this study are as follows:

- We present encouraging preliminary results on using authorship attribution approaches for uncovering real sockpuppet cases in Wikipedia. To the best of our knowledge, we are the first to tackle this problem.

- We identify novel features that have high discriminative power and are suitable for this task, where the input text is very short. These features can be helpful in other social media settings, as there are many shared characteristics across this genre.

The rest of the paper is organized as follows: in Section 2, we provide a detailed discussion on Wikipedia's editing environment and culture. In Section 3, we talk about authorship attribution and related work. Then in Section 4, we present our detailed approach. In Sections 5, 6, and 7, we discuss the data set, experimental setup, and results, respectively. Finally, we present an overall discussion and future directions in Sections 8 and 9.

## 2 Background

In Wikipedia, whenever a user acts in bad faith, vandalizes existing articles, or creates spurious articles, that user is banned from editing new content. The ban can last for some hours, to days, and in some cases it can be permanent. Sometimes, a banned user creates a new account to circumvent the ban, or edits Wikipedia without signing in.

These extra accounts or IP addresses, from which logged out edits are made, are called sockpuppets. The primary (oldest) account is called the sockpuppeteer. Whenever an editor is suspected to be a sockpuppet of another editor, a sockpuppet investigation case is filed against those accounts. Any editor can file a case, but the editor must provide supporting evidence as well. Typical evidence includes information about the editing actions related to those accounts, such as the articles, the topics, vandalism patterns, timing of account creation, timing of edits, and voting pattern in disagreements.

Sometime after the case is filed, an administrator will investigate the case. An administrator is an editor with privileges to make account management decisions, such as banning an editor. If the administrator is convinced that the suspect is a sockpuppet, he declares the verdict as confirmed. He also issues bans to the corresponding accounts and closes the case. If an administrator cannot reach a verdict on a case, he asks for a check user to intervene. Check users are higher privileged editors, who have access to private information regarding editors and edits, such as the IP address from which an editor has logged in. Other interested editors in the case, or the original editor who filed the case can also ask for a check user to intervene. The check user will review the evidence, as well as private information regarding the case, and will try to establish the connection between the sockpuppet and puppeteer. Then the check user will rule on the case. Finally, another administrator will look at the check user report and issue a final verdict. During the process, the accused editors, both the puppeteer and the sockpuppet, can submit evidence in their favor. But this additional evidence is not mandatory.

The current process to resolve suspected cases of sockpuppets has several disadvantages. We have already mentioned the first one. Because it is a manual process, it is time consuming and expensive. Perhaps a more serious weakness is the fact that relaying on IP addresses is not robust, as simple counter measures can fool the check users. An alternative to this process could be an automated framework that relies on the analysis of the comments to link editor accounts, as we propose in this paper.

## 3 Related Work

Modern approaches to AA typically follow a text classification framework where the classes are the set of candidate authors. Different machine learning algorithms have been used, including memory-based learners (Luyckx and Daelemans, 2008a; Luyckx and Daelemans, 2010), Support Vector Machines (Escalante et al., 2011), and Probabilistic Context Free Grammars (Raghavan et al., 2010).

Similarity-based approaches have also been successfully used for AA. In this setting, the training documents from the same author are concatenated into a single file to generate profiles from author-specific features. Then authorship predictions are based on similarity scores. (Keselj et al., 2003; Stamatatos, 2007; Koppel et al., 2011) are examples of successful examples of this approach.

Previous research has shown that low-level features, such as character n-grams are very powerful discriminators of writing styles. Although, enriching the models with other types of features can boost accuracy. In particular, stylistic features (punctuation marks, use of emoticons, capitalization information), syntactic information (at the part-of-speech level and features derived from shallow parsing), and even semantic features (bag-of-words) have shown to be useful.

Because of the difficulties in finding data from real cases, most of the published work in AA evaluates the different methods on data collections that were gathered originally for other purposes. Examples of this include the Reuters Corpus (Lewis et al., 2004) that has been used for benchmarking different approaches to AA (Stamatatos, 2008; Plakias and Stamatatos, 2008; Escalante et al., 2011) and the datasets used in the 2011 and 2012 authorship identification competitions from the PAN Workshop series (Argamon and Juola, 2011; Juola, 2012). Other researchers have invested efforts in creating their own AA corpus by eliciting written samples from subjects participating in their studies (Luyckx and Daelemans, 2008b; Goldstein-Stewart et al., 2008), or crawling though online websites (Narayanan et al., 2012).

In contrast, in this paper we focus on data from Wikipedia, where there is a real need to identify if the comments submitted by what appear to be different users, belong to a sockpuppeteer. Data from real world scenarios like this make solving the AA problem an even more urgent and practical matter, but also impose additional challenges to what is already a difficult problem. First, the texts analyzed in the Wikipedia setting were generated by people with the actual intention of deceiving the administrators into believing they are indeed coming from different people. With few exceptions (Afroz et al., 2012; Juola and Vescovi, 2010), most of the approaches to AA have been evaluated with data where the authors were not making a conscious effort to deceive or disguise their own identities or writeprint. Since there has been very little research done on deception detection, it is not well understood how AA approaches need to be adapted for these situations, or what kinds of features must be included to cope with deceptive writing. However, we do assume this adds a complicating factor to the task, and previous research has shown considerable decreases in AA accuracy when deception is present (Brennan and Greenstadt, 2009). Second, the length of the documents is usually shorter for the Wikipedia comments than that of other collections used. Document length will clearly affect the prediction performance of AA approaches, as the shorter documents will contain less information to develop author writeprint models and to make an inference on attribution. As we will describe later, this prompted us to reframe our solution in order to circumvent this short document length issue. Lastly, the data available is limited, there is an average of 80 entries per user in the training set from the collection we gathered, and an average of 8 messages in the test set, and this as well limits the amount of evidence available to train author models. Moreover, the test cases have an average of 8 messages. This is a very small amount of texts to make the final prediction.

## 4 Approach

In our framework, each comment made by a user is considered a "document" and therefore, each comment represents an instance of the classification task. There are two steps in our method. In the first step, we gather predictions from the classifier on each comment. Then in the second step we take the predictions for each comment and combine them in a majority voting schema to assign final decisions to each account.

The two step process we just described helps us deal with the challenging length of the individual comments. It is also an intuitive approach, since what we need to determine is if the account belongs to the sockpuppeteer. The ruling is at the account-level, which is also consistent with the human process. In the case of a positive prediction by our system, we take as a **confidence** measure on the predictions the percentage of comments that were individually predicted as sockpuppet cases.

### 4.1 Feature Engineering

In this study, we have selected typical features of authorship attribution, as well as new features we collected from inspecting the data by hand. In total, we have 239 features that capture stylistic, grammatical, and formatting preferences of the authors. The features are described below.

**Total number of characters:** The goal of this feature is to model the author's behavior of writing long wordy texts, or short comments.

**Total number of sentences:** We count the total number of sentences in the comments. While this feature is also trying to capture some preferences regarding the productivity of the author's comments, it can tell us more about the author's preference to organize the text in sentences. Some online users tend to write in long sentences and thus end up with a smaller number of sentences. To fragment the comments into sentences, we use the Lingua-EN-Sentence-0.25 from `www.cpan.org` (The Comprehensive Perl Archive Network). This off-the-shelf tool prevents abbreviations to be considered as sentence delimiters.

**Total number of tokens:** We define a token as any sequence of consecutive characters with no white spaces in between. Tokens can be words, numbers, numbers with letters, or with punctuation, such as *apple, 2345, 15th, and wow!!!*. For this feature we just count how many tokens are in the comment.

**Words without vowels:** Most English words have one or more vowels. The rate of words without vowels can also be a giveaway marker for some authors. Some words without vowels are *try, cry, fly, myth, gym,* and *hymn*.

**Total alphabet count:** This feature consists of the count of all the alphabetic characters used by the author in the text.

**Total punctuation count:** Some users use punctuation marks in very unique ways. For instance, semicolons and hyphens show noticeable differences in their use, some people avoid them completely, while others might use them in excess. Moreover, the use of commas is different in different parts of the world, and that too can help identify the author.

**Two/three continuous punctuation count:** Sequences of the same punctuation mark are often used to emphasize or to add emotion to the text, such as *wow!!!*, and *really??*. Signaling emotion in written text varies greatly for different authors. Not everyone displays emotions explicitly or feels comfortable expressing them in text. We believe this could also help link users to sockpuppet cases.

**Total contraction count:** Contractions are used for presenting combined words such as *don't*, *it's*, *I'm*, and *he's*. The contractions, or the spelled-out-forms are both correct grammatically. Hence, the use of contraction is somewhat a personal writing style attribute. Although the use of contractions varies across different genres, in social media they are commonly used.

**Parenthesis count:** This is a typical authorship attribution feature that depicts the rate at which authors use parenthesis in their comments.

**All caps letter word count:** This is a feature where we counted the number of tokens having all upper case letters. They are either abbreviations, or words presented with emphasis. Some examples are *USA*, or "this is *NOT* correct".

**Emoticons count:** Emoticons are pictorial representations of feelings, especially facial expressions with parenthesis, punctuation marks, and letters. They typically express the author's mood. Some commonly used emoticons are :) or :-) for happy face, :( for sad face, ;) for winking, :D for grinning, <3 for love/heart, :O for being surprised, and :P for being cheeky/tongue sticking out.

**Happy emoticons count:** As one of the most widely used emoticons, happy face was counted as a specific feature. Both :) and :-) were counted towards this feature.

**Sentence count without capital letter at the beginning:** Some authors start sentences with numbers or small letters. This feature captures that writing style. An example can be "1953 was the year, ..." or, "big, bald, and brass - all applies to our man".

**Quotation count:** This is an authorship attribution feature where usage of quotation is counted as a feature. When quoting, not everyone uses the quotation punctuation and hence quotation marks count may help discriminate some writers from others.

**Parts of speech (POS) tags frequency:** We took a total of 36 parts of speech tags from the Penn Treebank POS (Marcus et al., 1993) tag set into consideration. We ignored all tags related to punctuation marks as we have other features capturing these characters.

**Frequency of letters:** We compute the frequency of each of the 26 English letters in the alphabet. The count is normalized by the total number of non-white characters in the comment. This contributed 26 features to the feature set.

**Function words frequency:** It has been widely acknowledged that the rate of function words is a good marker of authorship. We use a list of function words taken from the function words in (Zheng et al., 2006). This list contributed 150 features to the feature set.

All the features described above have been used in previous work on AA. Following are the features that we found by manually inspecting the Wikipedia data set. All the features involving frequency counts are normalized by the length of the comment.

**Small "i" frequency:** We found the use of small "i" in place of capital "I" to be common for some authors. Interestingly, authors who made this mistake repeated it quite often.

**Full stop without white space frequency:** Not using white space after full stop was found quite frequently, and authors repeated it regularly.

**Question frequency:** We found that some authors use question marks more frequently than others. This is an idiosyncratic feature as we found some authors abuse the use of question marks for sentences that do not require question marks, or use multiple question marks where one question mark would suffice.

**Sentence with small letter frequency:** Some authors do not start a sentence with the first letter capitalized. This behavior seemed to be homogeneous, meaning an author with this habit will do it almost always, and across all of its sockpuppet accounts.

**Alpha, digit, uppercase, white space, and tab frequency:** We found that the distribution of these special groups of characters varies from author to author. It captures formatting preferences of text such as the use of "one" and "zero" in place of "1" and "0", and uppercase letters for every word.

**'A', and an error frequency:** Error with usage of "a", and "an" was quite common. Many authors tend to use "a" in place of "an", and vice versa. We used a simple rate of all "a" in front of words starting with vowel, or "an" in front of words starting with consonant.

**"he", and "she" frequency:** Use of "he", or "she" is preferential to each author. We found that the use of "he", or "she" by any specific author for an indefinite subject is consistent across different comments.

## 5 Data

We collected our data from cases filed by real users suspecting sockpupeteering in the English Wikipedia. Our collection consists of comments made by the accused sockpuppet and the suspected puppeteer in various talk pages. All the information about sockpuppet cases is freely available, together with information about the verdict from the administrators. For the negative examples, we also collected comments made by other editors in the comment threads of the same talk pages. For each comment, we also collected the time when the comment was posted as an extra feature. We used this time data to investigate if non-authorship features can contribute to the performance of our model, and to compare the performance of stylistic features and external user account information.

| **Class** | **Total** | **Avg. Msg. Train** | **Avg. Mesg. Test** |
|---|---|---|---|
| Sockpuppet | 41 | 88.75 | 8.5 |
| Non-sockpuppet | 36 | 77.3 | 7.9 |

Table 1: Distribution of True/False sockpuppet cases in the experimental data set. We show the average number of messages in train and test partitions for both classes.

Our dataset has two types of cases: confirmed sockpuppet, and rejected sockpuppet. The confirmed cases are those where the administrators have made final decisions, and their verdict confirmed the case as a true sockpuppet case. Alternatively, for the rejected sockpuppet cases, the administrator's verdict exonerates the suspect of all accusations. The distribution of different cases is given in Table 1.

Of the cases we have collected, one of the notable puppeteers is "-Inanna-". This editor was active in Wikipedia for a considerable amount of time, from December 2005 to April 2006. He also has a number of sockpuppet investigation cases against him. Table 2 shows excerpts from comments made by this editor on the accounts confirmed as sockpuppet. We highlight in boldface the features that are more noticeable as similar patterns between the different user accounts.

An important aspect of our current evaluation framework is the preprocessing of the data. We "cleansed" the data by removing content that was not written by the editor. The challenge we face is that Wikipedia does not have a defined structure for comments. We can get the difference of each modification in the history of a comment thread. However, not all modifications are comments. Some can be reverts (changing content back to an old version), or updates. Additionally, if an editor replies to more than one part of a thread in response to multiple com-

| **Comment from the sockpuppeteer: -Inanna-** |
|---|
| Mine was original and i have worked on it more than 4 hours**.I** have changed it many times by opinions**.L**ast one was accepted by all the users(except for khokhoi)**.I** have never used sockpuppets**.P**lease dont care Khokhoi,Tombseye and Latinus.They are changing all the articles about Turks.The most important and famous people are on my picture. |
| **Comment from the sockpuppet: Altau** |
| Hello**.I** am trying to correct uncited numbers in Battle of Sarikamis and Crimean War by resources but khoikhoi and tombseye always try to revert them**.C**ould you explain them there is no place for hatred and propagandas, please? |
| **Comment from the others: Khoikhoi** |
| Actually, my version WAS the original image. Ask any other user. Inanna's image was uploaded later, and was snuck into the page by Inanna's sockpuppet before the page got protected. The image has been talked about, and people have rejected Inanna's image (see above). |

Table 2: Sample excerpt from a single sockpuppet case. We show in boldface some of the stylistic features shared between the sockpuppeter and the sockpuppet.

| System | P | R | F | A (%) |
|---|---|---|---|---|
| B-1 | 0.53 | 1 | 0.69 | 53.24 |
| B-2 | 0.53 | 0.51 | 0.52 | 50.64 |
| Our System | **0.68** | **0.75** | **0.72** | **68.83** |

Table 3: Prediction performance for sockpuppet detection. Measures reported are Precision (P), Recall (R), F-measure (F), and Accuracy (A). B-1 is a simple baseline of the majority class and B-2 is a random baseline.

ments, or edits someone else's comments for any reason, there is no fixed structure to distinguish each action. Hence, though our initial data collector tool gathered a large volume of data, we could not use all of it as the preprocessing step was highly involved and required some manual intervention.

## 6 Experimental Setting

We used Weka (Witten and Frank, 2005) – a widely recognized free and open source data-mining tool, to perform the classification. For the purpose of this study, we chose Weka's implementation of Support Vector Machine (SVM) with default parameters.

To evaluate in a scenario similar to the real setting in Wikipedia, we process each sockpuppet case separately, we measure prediction performance, and then aggregate the results of each case. For example, we take data from a confirmed sockpuppet case and generate the training and test instances. The training data comes from the comments made by the suspected sockpuppeteer, while the test data comes from the comments contributed by the sockpuppet account(s). We include negative samples for these cases by collecting comments made on the same talk pages by editors not reported or suspected of sockpuppeteering. Similarly, to measure the false positive ratio of our approach, we performed experiments with confirmed non-sockpuppet editors that were also filed as potential sockpuppets in Wikipedia.

## 7 Results

The results of our experiments are shown in Table 3. For comparison purposes we show results of two simple baseline systems. **B-1** is the trivial classifier that predicts every case as sockpuppet (majority). **B-2** is the random baseline (coin toss). However as seen in the table, both baseline systems are outperformed by our system that reached an accuracy of 68%. B-1 reached an accuracy of 53% and B-2 of 50%.

For the miss-classified instances of confirmed sockpuppet cases, we went back to the original comment thread and the investigation pages to find out the sources of erroneous predictions for our system. We found investigation remarks for 4 cases. Of these 4 cases, 2 cases were tied on the predictions for the individual comments. We flip a coin in our system to break ties. From the other 2 cases, one has the neutral comment from administrators: "Possible", which indicates some level of uncertainty. The last one has comments that indicate a meat puppet. A meat puppet case involves two different real people where one is acting under the influence of the other. A reasonable way of taking advantage of the current system is to use the confidence measure to make predictions of the cases where our system has the highest confidence, or higher than some threshold, and let the administrators handle those cases that are more difficult for an automated approach.

We have also conducted an experiment to rank our feature set with the goal of identifying informative features. We used information gain as the ranking metric. A snapshot of the top 30 contributing features according to information gain is given in Table 4. We can see from the ranking that some of the top-contributing features are idiosyncratic features. Such features are white space frequency, beginning of the sentence without capital letter, and no white space between sentences. We can also infer from Table 4 that function word features (My, me, its, that, the, I, some, be, have, and since), and part of speech tags (VBG-Verb:gerund or present participle, CD-Cardinal number, VBP-Verb:non-3rd person singular present, NNP-Singular proper noun, MD-Modal, and RB-Adverb) are among the most highly ranked features. Function words have been identified as highly discriminative features since the earliest work on authorship attribution.

Finally, we conducted experiments with two edit timing features for 49 cases. These two features are edit time of the day in a 24 hour clock, and edit day of the week. We were interested in exploring if adding these non-stylistic features could contribute to classification performance. To compare performance of these non-authorship attribution features, we conducted the same experiments without these features. The results are shown in Table 5. We can see that average confidence of the classification, as well as F-measure goes up with the timing features. These timing features are easy to extract automatically, therefore they should be included in an automated approach like the one we propose here.

## 8 Discussion

The experiments presented in the previous section are encouraging. They show that with a relatively small set of automatically generated features, a machine learning algorithm can identify, with a reasonable performance, the true cases of sockpuppets in Wikipedia.

| **Features** |
|---|
| Whitespace frequency |
| Punctuation count |
| Alphabet count |
| Contraction count |
| Uppercase letter frequency |
| Total characters |
| Number of tokens |
| me |
| my |
| its |
| that |
| Beginning of the sentence without capital letter † |
| VBG-Verb:gerund or present participle |
| No white space between sentences † |
| the |
| Frequency of L |
| I |
| CD-Cardinal number |
| Frequency of F |
| VBP-Verb:non-3rd person singular present |
| Sentence start with small letter † |
| some |
| NNP-Singular proper noun |
| be |
| Total Sentences |
| MD-Modal |
| ? mark frequency |
| have |
| since |
| RB-Adverb |

Table 4: Ranking of the top 30 contributing features for the experimental data using information gain. Novel features from our experiment are denoted by †.

| **Features used** | **Confidence** | **F-measure** |
|---|---|---|
| All + timing features | 84.04% | 0.72 |
| All - timing features | 78.78% | 0.69 |

Table 5: Experimental result showing performance of the method with and without timing features for the problem of detecting sockpuppet cases. These results are on a subset of 49 cases.

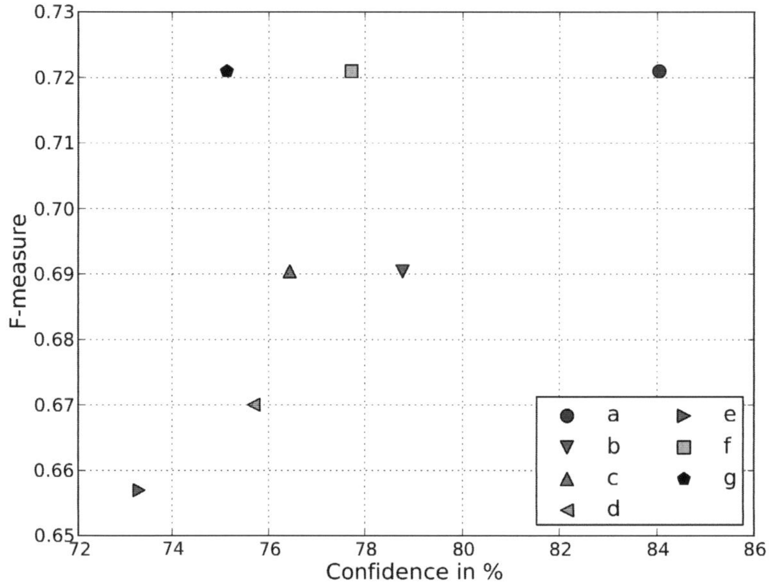


Figure 1: A plot of confidence in % for successful cases vs. F-measure for the system where we remove one feature group at a time. Here marker a) represents performance of the system with all the features. Markers b) timing features, c) part of speech tags, d) idiosyncratic features, e) function words, f) character frequencies, and g) AA features, represent performance of the system when the specified feature group is removed.

Since falsely accusing someone of using a sockpuppet could lead to serious credibility loss for users, we believe a system like ours could be used as a first pass in resolving the suspected sockpuppet cases, and bring into the loop the administrators for those cases where the certainty is not high.

To further investigate the contribution of different groups of features in our feature set, we conducted additional experiments where we remove one feature group at a time. Our goal is to see which feature group causes larger decreases in prediction performance when it is not used in the classification. We split our feature set into six groups, namely timing features, parts of speech tags, idiosyncratic features, function words, character frequencies, and authorship attribution features. In Figure 1, we show the result of the experiments. From the figure, we observe that function words are the most influential features as both confidence, and F-measure showed the largest drop when this group was excluded. The idiosyncratic features that we have included in the feature set showed the second largest decrease in prediction performance. Timing features, and part of speech tags have similar drops in F-measure but they showed a different degradation pattern on the confidence: part of speech tags caused the confidence to decrease by a larger margin than the timing features. Finally, character frequencies, and authorship attribution features did not affect F-measure much, but the confidence from the predictions did decrease considerably with AA features showing the second largest drop in confidence overall.

## 9 Conclusion and Future Directions

In this paper, we present a first attempt to develop an automated detection method of sockpuppets based solely on the publicly available comments from the suspected users. Sockpuppets have been a bane for Wikipedia as they are widely used by malicious users to subvert Wikipedia's editorial process and consensus. Our tool was inspired by recent work on the popular field of authorship attribution. It requires no additional administrative rights (e.g., the ability to view user IP addresses) and therefore can be used by regular users or administrators without check user rights. Our experimental evaluation with real sockpuppet cases from the English Wikipedia shows that our tool is a promising solution to the problem.

We are currently working on extending this study and improving our results. Specific aspects we would like to improve include a more robust confidence measure and a completely automated implementation. We are aiming to test our system on all the cases filed in the history of the English Wikipedia. Later on, it would be ideal to have a system like this running in the background and pro-actively scanning all active editors in Wikipedia, instead of running in a user triggered mode. Another useful extension would be to include other languages, as English is only one of the many languages currently represented in Wikipedia.

## Acknowledgements

This research was supported in part by ONR grant N00014-12-1-0217. The authors would like to thank the anonymous reviewers for their comments on a previous version of this paper.

## References

S. Afroz, M. Brennan, and R. Greenstadt. 2012. Detecting hoaxes, frauds, and deception in writing style online. In *Proceedings of the 2012 IEEE Symposium on Security and Privacy (S&P)*, pages 461–475. IEEE, May.

Shlomo Argamon and Patrick Juola. 2011. Overview of the international authorship identification competition at PAN-2011. In *Proceedings of the PAN 2011 Lab Uncovering Plagiarism, Authorship, and Social Software Misuse, held in conjunction with the CLEF 2011 Conference on Multilingual and Multimodal Information Access Evaluation*, Amsterdam.

M. Brennan and R. Greenstadt. 2009. Practical attacks against authorship recognition techniques. In *Proceedings of the Twenty-First Innovative Applications of Artificial Intelligence Conference.*

John Douceur. 2002. The Sybil attack. In Peter Druschel, Frans Kaashoek, and Antony Rowstron, editors, *Peer-to-Peer Systems*, volume 2429 of *Lecture Notes in Computer Science*, pages 251–260. Springer Berlin / Heidelberg.

H. J. Escalante, T. Solorio, and M. Montes-y Gómez. 2011. Local histograms of character n-grams for authorship attribution. In *Proceedings of the 49th Annual Meeting of the Association for Computational Linguistics: Human Language Technologies*, pages 288–298, Portland, Oregon, USA, June. Association for Computational Linguistics.

Jade Goldstein-Stewart, Kerri A. Goodwin, Roberta Evans Sabin, and Ransom K. Winder. 2008. Creating and using a correlated corpus to glean communicative commonalities. In *Proceedings of LREC-2008, the Sixth International Language Resources and Evaluation Conference.*

P. Juola and D. Vescovi. 2010. Empirical evaluation of authorship obfuscation using JGAAP. In *Proceedings of the 3rd ACM workshop on Artificial Intelligence and Security*, pages 14–18. ACM.

Patrick Juola. 2012. An overview of the traditional authorship attribution subtask. In *PAN 2012 Lab, Uncovering Plagiarism, Authorship and Social Software Misuse, held in conjunction with CLEF 2012.*

V. Keselj, F. Peng, N. Cercone, and C. Thomas. 2003. N-gram based author profiles for authorship attribution. In *Proceedings of the Pacific Association for Computational Linguistics*, pages 255–264.

Moshe Koppel, Jonathan Schler, and Shlomo Argamon. 2011. Authorship attribution in the wild. *Language Resources and Evaluation*, 45:83–94.

David D. Lewis, Yiming Yang, Tony G. Rose, and Fan Li. 2004. Rcv1: A new benchmark collection for text categorization research. *J. Mach. Learn. Res.*, 5:361–397, December.

Kim Luyckx and Walter Daelemans. 2008a. Authorship attribution and verification with many authors and limited data. In *Proceedings of the 22nd International Conference on Computational Linguistics (Coling 2008)*, pages 513–520, Manchester, UK, August.

Kim Luyckx and Walter Daelemans. 2008b. Personae: a corpus for author and personality prediction from text. In *Proceedings of LREC-2008, the Sixth International Language Resources and Evaluation Conference.*

Kim Luyckx and Walter Daelemans. 2010. The effect of author set size and data size in authorship attribution. *Literary and Linguistic Computing*, pages 1–21, August.

Mitchell P. Marcus, Mary Ann Marcinkiewicz, and Beatrice Santorini. 1993. Building a large annotated corpus of English: the Penn treebank. *Comput. Linguist.*, 19(2):313–330, June.

A. Narayanan, H. Paskov, N.Z. Gong, J. Bethencourt, E. Stefanov, E.C.R. Shin, and D. Song. 2012. On the feasibility of internet-scale author identification. In *Proceedings of the 33rd conference on IEEE Symposium on Security and Privacy*, pages 300–314. IEEE.

S. Plakias and E. Stamatatos. 2008. Tensor space models for authorship attribution. In *Proceedings of the 5th Hellenic Conference on Artificial Intelligence: Theories, Models and Applications*, volume 5138 of *LNCS*, pages 239–249, Syros, Greece.

Sindhu Raghavan, Adriana Kovashka, and Raymond Mooney. 2010. Authorship attribution using probabilistic context-free grammars. In *Proceedings of the 48th Annual Meeting of the ACL 2010*, pages 38–42, Uppsala, Sweden, July. Association for Computational Linguistics.

E. Stamatatos. 2007. Author identification using imbalanced and limited training texts. In *Proceedings of the 18th International Workshop on Database and Expert Systems Applications, DEXA '07*, pages 237–241, Sept.

E. Stamatatos. 2008. Author identification: Using text sampling to handle the class imbalance problem. *Information Processing and Managemement*, 44:790–799.

I. H. Witten and E. Frank. 2005. *Data Mining: Practical Machine Learning Tools and Techniques*. Morgan Kauffmann, 2nd edition.

Rong Zheng, Jiexun Li, Hsinchun Chen, and Zan Huang. 2006. A framework for authorship identification of online messages: Writing-style features and classification techniques. *Journal of the American Society for Information Science and Technology*, 57(3):378–393.

# Towards the Detection of Reliable Food-Health Relationships

**Michael Wiegand** and **Dietrich Klakow**
Spoken Language Systems
Saarland University
D-66123 Saarbrücken, Germany
{Michael.Wiegand|Dietrich.Klakow}@lsv.uni-saarland.de

## Abstract

We investigate the task of detecting reliable statements about food-health relationships from natural language texts. For that purpose, we created a specially annotated web corpus from forum entries discussing the healthiness of certain food items. We examine a set of task-specific features (mostly) based on linguistic insights that are instrumental in finding utterances that are commonly perceived as reliable. These features are incorporated in a supervised classifier and compared against standard features that are widely used for various tasks in natural language processing, such as bag of words, part-of speech and syntactic parse information.

## 1 Introduction

In this paper, we explore some linguistic high-level features to detect food-health relationships in natural language texts that are perceived reliable. By food-health relationships we mean relations that claim that a food item is suitable (1) or unsuitable (2) for some particular health condition.

(1) *Baking soda* is an approved remedy against heartburn.

(2) During pregnancy women should not consume any *alcohol*.

The same health claim may be uttered in different ways (3)-(5) and, as a consequence, may be perceived and judged differently. For the automatic extraction of health claims, we believe that statements that are perceived as *reliable* (4)-(5) are the most important to retrieve.

(3) *Eggs* do not have a negative impact on people suffering from heart diseases.

(4) **According to a leading medical scientist**, the consumption of *eggs* does not have a negative impact on people suffering from heart diseases.

(5) I'm suffering from a heart disease and **all my life** I've been eating many *eggs*; it never had any impact on my well-being.

In this work, we will mine a web corpus of forum entries for such relations. Social media are a promising source of such knowledge as, firstly, the language employed is not very technical and thus, unlike medical texts, accessible to the general public. Secondly, social media can be considered as an exclusive repository of *popular wisdom*. With regard to the health conditions, we can find, for example, home remedies. Despite the fact that many of them are not scientifically proven, there is still a great interest in that type of knowledge. However, even though such content is usually not subject to any scientific review, users would appreciate an automatic assessment of the quality of each relation expressed. In this work, we attempt a first step towards this endeavour by automatically classifying these utterances with regard to *reliability*.

The features we examine will be (mostly) based on linguistic insights that are instrumental in finding utterances that are commonly perceived as reliable. These features are incorporated in a supervised classifier and compared against standard features that are widely used for various tasks in natural language processing, such as bag of words, part-of speech and syntactic parse information.

Our experiments are carried out on German data. We believe, however, that our findings carry over to other languages since the linguistic aspects that we address are (mostly) language universal. For the sake of general accessibility, all examples will be given as English translations.

## 2 Related Work

As far as the extraction of health relations from social media are concerned, the prediction of epidemics (Fisichella et al., 2011; Torii et al., 2011; Diaz-Aviles et al., 2012; Munro et al., 2012) has recently attracted the attention of the research community.

Relation extraction involving food items has also been explored in the context of ontology alignment (van Hage et al., 2005; van Hage et al., 2006; van Hage et al., 2010) and also as a means of knowledge acquisition for virtual customer advice in a supermarket (Wiegand et al., 2012a).

The works most closely related to this paper are Yang et al. (2011) and Miao et al. (2012). Both of these works address the extraction of food-health relationships. Unlike this work, they extract relations from scientific biomedical texts rather than social media. Yang et al. (2011) also cover the task of *strength analysis* which bears some resemblance to the task of finding reliable utterances to some extent. However, the features applied to that classification task are only standard features, such as bag of words.

## 3 Data & Annotation

As a corpus for our experiments, we used a crawl of *chefkoch.de*[1] (Wiegand et al., 2012a) consisting of 418,558 webpages of food-related forum entries. *chefkoch.de* is the largest web portal for food-related issues in the German language. From this dataset, sentences in which some food item co-occurred with some health condition (e.g. *pregnancy*, *diarrhoea* or *flu*) were extracted. (In the following, we will also refer to these entities as *target food item* and *target health condition*.) The food items were identified with the help of GermaNet (Hamp and Feldweg, 1997), the German version of WordNet (Miller et al., 1990), and the health conditions were used from Wiegand et al. (2012b). In total, 2604 sentences were thus obtained.

For the manual annotation, each target sentence (i.e. a sentence with a co-occurrence of target food item and health condition) was presented in combination with the two sentences immediately preceding and following it. Each target sentence was manually assigned two labels, one specifying the type of suitability (§3.1) and another specifying whether the relation expressed is considered reliable or not (§3.2).

### 3.1 Types of Suitability

The suitability-label indicates whether a polar relationship holds between the target food item and the target health condition, and if so, which. Rather than just focusing on positive polarity, i.e. suitability, and negative polarity, i.e. unsuitability, we consider more fine-grained classes. As such, the suitability-label does not provide any explicit information about the reliability of the utterance. In principle, every polar relationship between target food item and health condition expressed in a text could also be formulated in such a way that it is perceived reliable. In this work, we will consider the suitability-label as given. We use it as a feature in order to measure the correlation between suitability and reliability. The usage of fine-grained labels is to investigate whether subclasses of suitability or unsuitability have a tendency to co-occur with reliability. (In other words: we may assume differences among labels with the same polarity type.) We define the following set of fine-grained suitability-labels:

#### 3.1.1 Suitable (SUIT)

SUIT encompasses all those statements in which the consumption of the target food item is claimed to be suitable for people affected by a particular health condition (6). By *suitable*, we mean that there will not be a negative effect on the health of a person once he or she consumes the target food item. However, this relation type does not state that the consumption is likely to improve the condition of the person either.

(6) I also got <u>dermatitis</u> which is why my mother used *spelt flour* [instead of wheat flour]; you don't taste a difference.

[1] www.chefkoch.de

| positive labels | BENEF, SUIT, PREVENT |
|---|---|
| negative labels | UNSUIT, CAUSE |

Table 1: Categorization of suitability-labels.

#### 3.1.2 Beneficial (BENEF)

While SUIT only states that the consumption of the target food item is suitable for people with a particular health condition, BENEF actually states that the consumption alleviates the symptoms of the condition or even cures it (7). While both SUIT and BENEF have a positive polarity, SUIT is much more neutral than BENEF.

(7) Usually, a glass of *milk* helps me when I got a sore throat.

#### 3.1.3 Prevention (PREVENT)

An even stronger positive effect than the relation type BENEF presents PREVENT which claims that the consumption of the target food item can prevent the outbreak of a particular disease (8).

(8) *Citric acid* largely reduces the chances of kidney stones to develop.

#### 3.1.4 Unsuitable (UNSUIT)

UNSUIT describes cases in which the consumption of the target food item is deemed unsuitable (9). Unsuitability means that one expects a negative effect (but it need not be mentioned explicitly), that is, a deterioration of the health situation on the part of the person who is affected by a particular health condition.

(9) *Raw milk cheese* should not be eaten during pregnancy.

#### 3.1.5 Causation (CAUSE)

CAUSE is the negative counterpart of PREVENT. It states that the consumption of the target food item can actually cause a particular health condition (10).

(10) It's a common fact that the regular consumption of *coke* causes caries.

The suitability-labels can also be further separated into two polar classes (i.e. positive and negative labels) as displayed in Table 1.

### 3.2 Reliability

Each utterance was additionally labeled as to whether it was considered reliable (4)-(5) or not (3). It is this label that we try to predict in this work. By *reliable*, we understand utterances in which the relations expressed are convincing in the sense that a reputable source is cited, some explanation or empirical evidence for the relation is given, or the relation itself is emphasized by the speaker. In this work, we are exclusively interested in detecting utterances which are *perceived* reliable by the reader. We leave aside whether the statements from our text corpus are actually correct. Our aim is to identify linguistic cues that evoke the impression of *reliability* on behalf of the reader.

### 3.3 Class Distributions and Annotation Agreement

Table 2 depicts the distribution of the reliability-labels on our corpus while Table 3 lists the class distribution of the suitability-labels including the proportion of the reliable instances among each category. The proportion of reliable instances varies quite a lot among the different suitability-labels, which indicates that the suitability may be some effective feature.

Note that the class OTHER in Table 3 comprises all instances in which the co-occurrence of a health condition and a food item was co-incidental (11) or there was some embedding that discarded the validity of the respective suitability-relation, as it is the case, for example, in questions (12).

(11) It's not his diabetes I'm concerned about but the enormous amounts of *fat* that he consumes.

(12) Does anyone know whether I can eat *tofu* during my pregnancy?

In order to measure interannotation agreement, we collected for three health conditions their co-occurrences with any food item. For the suitability-labels we computed Cohen's $\kappa = 0.76$ and for the reliability-labels $\kappa = 0.61$. The agreement for reliability is lower than for suitability. We assume that the reason for that lies in the highly subjective notion of reliability. Still, both agreements can be interpreted as *substantial* (Landis and Koch, 1977) and should be sufficiently high for our experiments.

| Type | Frequency | Percentage |
|---|---|---|
| Reliable | 480 | 18.43 |
| Not Reliable | 2124 | 81.57 |

Table 2: Distribution of the reliability-labels.

| Type | Frequency | Perc. | Perc. Reliable |
|---|---|---|---|
| BENEF | 502 | 19.28 | 33.39 |
| CAUSE | 482 | 18.51 | 22.57 |
| SUIT | 428 | 16.44 | 17.91 |
| UNSUIT | 277 | 10.64 | 34.05 |
| PREVENT | 74 | 2.84 | 14.04 |
| OTHER | 841 | 32.30 | 0.00 |

Table 3: Distribution of the suitability-labels.

# 4 Feature Design

## 4.1 Task-specific High-level Feature Types

We now describe the different task-specific high-level feature types. We call them *high-level* feature types since they model concepts that typically generalize over sets of individual words (i.e. low-level features).

### 4.1.1 Explanatory Statements (EXPL)

The most obvious type of reliability is a suitability-relation that is also accompanied by some explanatory statement. That is, some reason for the relation expressed is given (13). We detect reasons by scanning a sentence for typical discourse cues (more precisely: conjunctions) that anchor such remarks, e.g. *which is why* or *because*.

(13) *Honey* has an antiseptic effect **which is why** it is an ideal additive to milk in order to cure a sore throat.

### 4.1.2 Frequent Observation (FREQ)

If a speaker claims to have witnessed a certain relation very frequently or even at all times, then there is a high likelihood that this relation actually holds (14). We use a set of adverbs (18 expressions) that express high frequency (e.g. *often*, *frequently* etc.) or constancy (e.g. *always*, *at all times* etc.).

(14) What **always** helps me when I have the flu is a hot *chicken broth*.

### 4.1.3 Intensifiers (INTENS)

Some utterances may also be perceived reliable if their speaker adds some emphasis to them. One way of doing so is by adding intensifiers to a remark (15).

(15) You can treat nausea with *ginger* **very effectively**.

The intensifiers we use are a translation of the lexicon introduced in Wilson et al. (2005). For the detection, we divide that list into two groups:

The first group $\text{INTENS}_{simple}$ are unambiguous adverbs that always function as intensifiers no matter in which context they appear (e.g. *very* or *extremely*).

The second group includes more ambiguous expressions, such as adjectives that only function as an intensifier if they modify a polar expression (e.g. *horrible pain* or *terribly nice*) otherwise they function as typical polar expressions (e.g. *you are horrible*$^-$ or *he sang terribly*$^-$). We employ two methods to detect these ambiguous expressions. $\text{INTENS}_{polar}$ requires a polar expression of a polarity lexicon to be modified by the intensifier, while $\text{INTENS}_{adj}$ requires an adjective to be modified. In order to identify polar expressions we use the polarity lexicon underlying the *PolArt* system (Klenner et al., 2009). We also consider adjectives since we must assume that our polarity lexicon does not cover all possible polar expressions. We chose adjectives as a complement criterion as this part of speech is known to contain most polar expressions (Hatzivassiloglou and McKeown, 1997; Hatzivassiloglou and Wiebe, 2000).

### 4.1.4 Strong Polar Expressions (STROPO)

Instead of adding intensifiers in order to put more emphasis to a remark (§4.1.3), one may also use polar expressions that convey a high polar intensity (16). For instance, *nice* and *excellent* refer to the same scale and convey positive polarity but *excellent* has a much higher polar intensity than *nice*. Taboada et al. (2011) introduced an English polarity lexicon *SO-CAL* in which polar expressions were also assigned an intensity label. As our German polarity lexicon (§4.1.3) does not contain comparable intensity labels, we used a German translation of *SO-CAL*. We identified polar expressions with a high intensity score (i.e. $\pm 4$ or $\pm 5$) as *strong polar expressions*. It includes 221 highly positive and 344 highly negative polar expressions. We also distinguish the polarity type (i.e. $\text{STROPO}^+$ refers to positive and $\text{STROPO}^-$ refers to negative polarity).

(16) *Baking soda* is an **excellent** remedy against heartburn.

#### 4.1.5 Superlatives (SUPER)

Another way of expressing high polar intensity is by applying superlatives (17). Superlatives can only be formed from gradable adjectives. At the same time, the greatest amount of such adjectives are also subjective expressions (Hatzivassiloglou and Wiebe, 2000). As a consequence, the detection of this grammatical category does not depend on a subjectivity/polarity lexicon but on simple morphological suffixes (e.g. *-est* in *strongest*)[2] or combinations with certain modifiers (e.g. *most* in *most terrific*).

(17) *Baking soda* is the **most effective** remedy against heartburn.

#### 4.1.6 Statements Made by Authorities (AUTH)

If a statement is quoted from an authority, then it is usually perceived more reliable than other statements (4). Authorities in our domain are mostly scientists and medical doctors. Not only does a mention of those types of professions indicate an authority but also the citation of their work. Therefore, for this feature we also scan for expressions, such as *journal*, *report*, *survey* etc. Our final look-up list of cues comprises 53 expressions.

We also considered using the knowledge of user profiles in order to identify speakers whose profession fall under our defined set of authorities. Unfortunately, the overwhelming majority of users who actually specified their profession cannot be considered as authorities (for the relations that we are interested in) by mere consideration of their profession. Most users of *chefkoch.de* are either office employees, housewifes, students or chefs. Less than 1% are authorities according to our definition. Due to the severe sparsity of authorities, we refrained from using the professions as they are specified in the user profiles.

[2]We could not use part-of-speech tagging for the detection of superlatives since, unlike the standard English part-of-speech tag set (i.e. the Penn Treebank Tag Set (Marcus et al., 1993)), information regarding gradation (i.e. comparative and superlative) is not reflected in the standard German tag set (i.e. Stuttgart Tübinger Tag Set (Schiller et al., 1995)).

#### 4.1.7 Doctors' Prescriptions (PRESC)

Some of our food-health relations are also mentioned in the context of doctors' prescriptions (5). That is, a doctor may prescribe a patient to consume a particular food item since it is considered suitable for their health condition, or he/she may forbid a food item in case it is considered unsuitable. As already pointed out in §4.1.6, doctors usually present an authority with regard to food-health relations. That is why, their remarks should be considered reliable.

In order to detect doctors' prescriptions, we mainly look for (modal) verbs in a sentence that express obligations or prohibitions. We found that, on our dataset, people rarely mention their doctor explicitly if they refer to a particular prescription. Instead, they just mention that they must or must not consume a particular food item. From the context, however, it is obvious that they refer to their doctor's prescription (18).

(18) Due to my diabetes I **must** not eat any *sweets*.

#### 4.1.8 Hedge Cues (HEDGE)

While all previous features were designed to identify cases of reliable statements, we also include features that indicate the opposite. The most obvious type of utterances that are commonly considered unreliable are so-called *hedges* (Lakoff, 1973) or speculations (19).

(19) *Coke* **may** cause cancer.

For this feature, we use a German translation of English cue words that have been found useful in previous work (Morante and Daelemans, 2009) which results in 47 different expressions.

#### 4.1.9 Types of Suitability-Relations (REL)

Finally, we also incorporate the information about what type of suitability-relation a statement was labeled with. The suitability-labels were already presented and motivated in §3.1. The concrete features are: $\text{REL}_{SUIT}$ (§3.1.1), $\text{REL}_{BENEF}$ (§3.1.2), $\text{REL}_{PREVENT}$ (§3.1.3), $\text{REL}_{UNSUIT}$ (§3.1.4), $\text{REL}_{CAUSE}$ (§3.1.5).

| Suffix | Description |
|---|---|
| -WND$_{food}$ | context window around food item |
| -WND$_{cond}$ | context window around health condition |
| -TS | target sentence only |
| -EC | entire (instance) context |

Table 4: Variants for the individual feature types.

### 4.2 Variants of Feature Types

For our feature types we examine several variants that differ in the size of context/scope. We distinguish between the target sentence and the entire context of an instance, i.e. the target sentence plus the two preceding and following sentences (§3). If only the target sentence is considered, we can also confine the occurrence of a cue word to a fixed window (comprising 5 words) either around the target food item or the target health condition rather than considering the entire sentence.

Small contexts usually offer a good precision. For example, if a feature type occurs nearby a mention of the target food item or health condition, the feature type and the target expression are likely to be related to each other. The downside of such narrow contexts is that they may be too sparse. Wide contexts may be better suited to situations in which a high recall is desirable. However, ambiguous feature types may perform poorly with these contexts as their co-occurrence with a target expression at a large distance is likely to be co-incidental.

Table 4 lists all the variants that we use. These variants are applied to all feature types except the types of suitability (§4.1.9) as this label has only been assigned to an entire target sentence.

### 4.3 Other Features

Table 5 lists the entire set of features that we examine in this work. The simplest classifier that we can construct for our task is a trivial classifier that predicts all statements as reliable statements. The remaining features comprise bag of words, part-of-speech and syntactic parse information. For the latter two features, we employ the output of the Stanford Parser for German (Rafferty and Manning, 2008).

| Features | Description |
|---|---|
| all | trivial classifier that always predicts a reliable statement |
| bow | bag-of-words features: all words between the target food item and target health condition and the words immediately preceding and following each of them |
| pos | part-of-speech features: part-of-speech sequence between target food item and health condition and tags of the words immediately preceding and following each of the target expressions |
| synt | path from syntactic parse tree from target food item to target health condition |
| task | all task-specific high-level feature types from §4.1 with their respective variants (§4.2) |

Table 5: Description of all feature sets.

## 5 Experiments

Each instance to be classified is a sentence in which there is a co-occurrence of a target food item and a target health condition along its respective context sentences (§3). We only consider sentences in which the co-occurrence expresses an actual suitability relationship between the target food item and the target health condition, that is, we ignore instances labeled with the suitability-label OTHER (§3.3). We make this restriction as the instances labeled as OTHER are not eligible for being reliable statements (Table 3). In this work, we take the suitability-labels for granted (this allows us to easily exclude the instances labeled as OTHER). The automatic detection of suitability-labels would require a different classifier with a different set of features whose appropriate discussion would be beyond the scope of this paper.

### 5.1 Comparison of the Different Task-specific High-level Features

In our first experiment, we want to find out how the different task-specific high-level features that we have proposed in this work compare to each other. More specifically, we want to find out how the individual features correlate with the utterances that have been manually marked as reliable. For that purpose, Table 6 shows the top 20 features according to Chi-square feature selection computed with *WEKA* (Witten and Frank, 2005). More information regarding the computation of Chi-square statistics in the context of text classification can be found in Yang and Pederson (1997). Note that we apply feature selection only as a means of feature compar-

| Rank | Feature | Score |
|---|---|---|
| 1 | **FREQ-WND**$_{food}$ | 105.1 |
| 2 | FREQ-TS | 102.8 |
| 3 | FREQ-WND$_{cond}$ | 75.9 |
| 4 | FREQ-EC | 29.2 |
| 5 | **AUTH-EC** | 23.7 |
| 6 | **STROPO**$^{+}$**-WND**$_{cond}$ | 20.5 |
| 7 | **REL**$_{BENEF}$ | 20.2 |
| 8 | REL$_{SUIT}$ | 16.8 |
| 9 | **INTENS**$_{simple}$**-WND**$_{cond}$ | 16.4 |
| 10 | AUTH-TS | 15.4 |
| 11 | STROPO$^{+}$-TS | 15.0 |
| 12 | INTENS$_{simple}$-EC | 14.1 |
| 13 | STROPO$^{+}$-WND$_{food}$ | 13.7 |
| 14 | INTENS$_{adj}$-WND$_{food}$ | 13.2 |
| 15 | INTENS$_{simple}$-WND$_{food}$ | 12.1 |
| 16 | INTENS$_{simple}$-TS | 11.6 |
| 17 | **PRESC-WND**$_{food}$ | 11.0 |
| 18 | INTENS$_{adj}$-WND$_{cond}$ | 9.7 |
| 19 | INTENS$_{polar}$-EC | 9.0 |
| 20 | AUTH-WND$_{food}$ | 7.9 |

Table 6: Top 20 features according to Chi-square feature ranking (for each feature type the most highly ranked variant is highlighted).

ison. For classification (§5.2), we will use the entire feature set.

### 5.1.1 What are the most effective features?

There are basically five feature types that dominate the highest ranks. They are FREQ, AUTH, STROPO, REL and INTENS. This already indicates that several features presented in this work are effective. It is interesting to see that two types of suitability-labels, i.e. REL$_{BENEF}$ and REL$_{SUIT}$, are among the highest ranked features which suggests that suitability and reliability are somehow connected.

Table 7 shows both precision and recall for each of the most highly ranked variant of the feature types that appear on the top 20 ranks according to Chi-square ranking (Table 6). Thus, we can have an idea in how far the high performing feature types differ. We only display one feature per feature type due to the limited space. The table shows that for most of these features precision largely outperforms recall. REL$_{BENEF}$ is the only notable exception (its recall actually outperforms precision).

### 5.1.2 Positive Orientation and Reliability

By closer inspection of the highly ranked features, we found quite a few features with positive orientation, i.e. STROPO$^{+}$-WND$_{cond}$, REL$_{BENEF}$, REL$_{SUIT}$, STROPO$^{+}$-WND$_{cond}$, while their negative counterparts are absent. This raises the question whether there is a bias for positive orientation for the detection of reliability.

| Feature | Prec | Rec |
|---|---|---|
| FREQ-WND$_{food}$ | 71.13 | 14.38 |
| AUTH-EC | 41.81 | 15.42 |
| STROPO$^{+}$-WND$_{cond}$ | 63.38 | 3.54 |
| REL$_{BENEF}$ | 33.39 | 39.17 |
| INTENS$_{simple}$-WND$_{cond}$ | 41.73 | 11.04 |
| PRESC-WND$_{food}$ | 45.00 | 5.63 |

Table 7: Precision and recall of different features (we list the most highly ranked variants of the feature types from Table 6).

We assume that there are different reasons why the positive suitability-labels (REL$_{BENEF}$ and REL$_{SUIT}$) and strong positive polarity (STROPO$^{+}$) are highly ranked features:

As far as polarity features are concerned, it is known from sentiment analysis that positive polarity is usually easier to detect than negative polarity (Wiegand et al., 2013). This can largely be ascribed to social conventions to be less blunt with communicating negative sentiment. For that reason, for example, one often applies negated positive polar expressions (e.g. *not okay*) or irony to express a negative sentiment rather than using an explicit negative polar expression. Of course, such implicit types of negative polarity are much more difficult to detect automatically.

The highly ranked suitability-labels may be labels with the same orientation (i.e. they both describe relationships that a food item is suitable rather than unsuitable for a particular health condition), yet they have quite different properties.[3] While REL$_{BENEF}$ is a feature positively correlating with reliable utterances, the opposite is true of REL$_{SUIT}$, that is, there is a correlation but this correlation is negative. Table 8 compares their respective precision and also includes the trivial (reference) classifier *all* that always predicts a reliable statement. The table clearly shows that REL$_{BENEF}$ is above the triv-

[3]It is not the case that the proportion of reliable utterances is larger among the entire set of instances tagged with positive suitability-labels than among the instances tagged with negative suitability-labels (Table 1). In both cases, they are at approx. 26%.

ial feature while $\text{REL}_{SUIT}$ is clearly below. (One may wonder why the gap in precision between those different features is not larger. These features are also high-recall features – we have shown this for $\text{REL}_{BENEF}$ in Table 7 – so the smaller gaps may already have a significant impact.) In plain, this result means that a statement conveying that some food item alleviates the symptoms of a particular disease or even cures it ($\text{REL}_{BENEF}$) is more likely to be an utterance that is perceived reliable rather than statements in which the speaker merely states that the food item is suitable given a particular health condition ($\text{REL}_{SUIT}$). Presumably, the latter type of suitability-relations are mostly uttered parenthetically (not emphatically), or they are remarks in which the relation is inferred, so that they are unlikely to provide further background information. In Sentence (20), for example, the suitability of *wholemeal products* is inferred as the speaker's father eats these types of food due to his *diabetes*. The focus of this remark, however, is the psychic well-being of the speaker's father. That entire utterance does not present any especially reliable or otherwise helpful information regarding the relationship between *diabetes* and *wholemeal products*.

(20) My father suffers from diabetes and is fed up with eating all these *wholemeal products*. We are worried that he is going to fall into a depression.

Having explained that the two (frequently occurring) positive suitability-labels are highly ranked features because they separate reliable from less reliable statements, one may wonder why we do not find a similar behaviour on the negative suitability-labels. The answer to this lies in the fact that there is no similar distinction between $\text{REL}_{BENEF}$ and $\text{REL}_{SUIT}$ among utterances expressing unsuitability. There is no neutral negative suitability-label similar to $\text{REL}_{SUIT}$. The relation $\text{REL}_{UNSUIT}$ expresses unsuitability which is usually connected with some deterioration in health.

#### 5.1.3 How important are explanatory statements for this task?

We were very surprised that the feature type to indicate explanatory statements EXPL (§4.1.1) performed very poorly (none of its variants is listed in Table 6) since we assumed explanatory statements to be one of the most relevant types of utterances. In order to find a reason for this, we manually annotated all reliable utterances as to whether they can be regarded as an explanatory statement ($\text{EXPL}_{all}$) and, if so, whether (in principle) there are lexical cues (such as our set of conjunctions) to identify them ($\text{EXPL}_{cue}$). Table 9 shows the proportion of these two categories among the reliable utterances. With more than $20\%$ being labeled as this subtype, explanatory statements are clearly not a fringe phenomenon. However, lexical cues could only be observed in approximately $1/3$ of those instances. The majority of cases, such as Sentence (21), do not contain any lexical cues and are thus extremely difficult to detect.

| **Feature** | $\text{REL}_{SUIT}$ | *all* | $\text{REL}_{BENEF}$ |
|---|---|---|---|
| **Prec** | 17.81 | 26.46 | 33.39 |

Table 8: The precision of different REL-features compared to the trivial classifier *all* that always predicts a reliable utterance.

| **Type** | $\text{EXPL}_{all}$ | $\text{EXPL}_{cue}$ |
|---|---|---|
| **Percentage** | 22.59 | 8.30 |

Table 9: Proportion of explanatory statements among reliable utterances ($\text{EXPL}_{all}$: all reliable instances that are explanatory statements; $\text{EXPL}_{cue}$: subset of explanatory statements that also contain a lexical cue).

(21) *Citrus fruits* are bad for dermatitis. They increase the itch. Such fruits are rich in acids that irritate your skin.

In addition, all variants of our feature type EXPL have a poor precision (between $20-25\%$). This means that the underlying lexical cues are too ambiguous.

#### 5.1.4 How important are the different contextual scopes?

Table 6 clearly shows that the contextual scope of a feature type matters. For example, for the feature type FREQ, the most effective scope achieves a Chi-square score of 105.1 while the worst variant only achieves a score of 29.2. However, there is no unique contextual scope which always outperforms the other variants. This is mostly due to the

| Feature Set | Prec | Rec | F1 |
|---|---|---|---|
| all | 26.46 | **100.00** | 41.85 |
| bow | 37.14 | 62.44 | 46.45 |
| bow+pos | 36.85 | 57.64 | 44.88 |
| bow+synt | 39.05 | 58.01 | 46.58 |
| task | 35.16 | 72.89 | 47.21 |
| bow+task | **42.54** | 66.01 | **51.56***|

Table 10: Comparison of different feature sets (summary of features is displayed in Table 5); * significantly better than *bow* at $p < 0.05$ (based on paired t-test).

fact the different feature types have different properties. On the one hand, there are unambiguous feature types, such as AUTH, which work fine with a wide scope. But we also have ambiguous feature types that require a fairly narrow context. A typical example are strong (positive) polar expressions (STROPO$^+$). (Polar expressions are known to be very ambiguous (Wiebe and Mihalcea, 2006; Akkaya et al., 2009).)

### 5.2 Classification

Table 10 compares the different feature sets with regard to extraction performance. We carry out a 5-fold cross-validation on our manually labeled dataset. As a classifier, we chose Support Vector Machines (Joachims, 1999). As a toolkit, we use *SVMLight*[4] with a linear kernel.

Table 10 clearly shows the strength of the high-level features that we proposed. They do not only represent a strong feature set on their own but they can also usefully be combined with bag-of-words features. Apparently, neither part-of-speech nor parse information are predictive for this task.

### 5.3 Impact of Training Data

Figure 1 compares bag-of-words features and our task-specific high-level features on a learning curve. The curve shows that the inclusion of our task-specific features improves performance. Interestingly, with *task* alone we obtain a good performance on smaller amounts of data. However, this classifier is already saturated with 40% of the training data. From then onwards, it is more effective to use the combination *bow+task*. Our high-level features generalize well which is particularly important for situations in which only few training data are available.

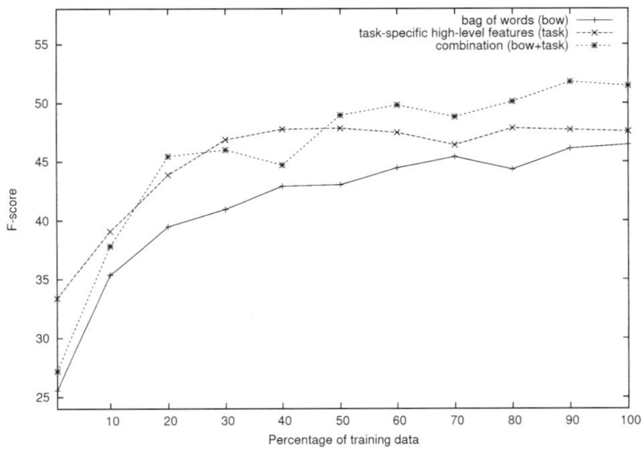


Figure 1: Learning curve of the different feature sets.

However, in situations in which large training sets are available, we additionally need bag of words that are able to harness more sparse but specific information.

## 6 Conclusion

In this paper, we examined a set of task-specific high-level features in order to detect food-health relations that are perceived reliable. We found that, in principle, a subset of these features that include adverbials expressing frequent observations, statements made by authorities, strong polar expressions and intensifiers are fairly predictive and complement bag-of-words information. We also observed a correlation between some suitability-labels and reliability. Moreover, the effectiveness of the different features depends very much on the context to which they are applied.

## Acknowledgements

This work was performed in the context of the Software-Cluster project EMERGENT. Michael Wiegand was funded by the German Federal Ministry of Education and Research (BMBF) under grant no. "01IC10S01". The authors would like to thank Stephanie Köser for annotating the dataset presented in the paper. The authors would also like to thank Prof. Dr. Wolfgang Menzel for providing the German version of the SO-CAL polarity lexicon that has been developed at his department.

[4]`http://svmlight.joachims.org`

## References


Cem Akkaya, Janyce Wiebe, and Rada Mihalcea. 2009. Subjectivity Word Sense Disambiguation. In *Proceedings of the Conference on Empirical Methods in Natural Language Processing (EMNLP)*, pages 190–199, Singapore.

Ernesto Diaz-Aviles, Avar Stewart, Edward Velasco, Kerstin Denecke, and Wolfgang Nejdl. 2012. Epidemic Intelligence for the Crowd, by the Crowd. In *Proceedings of the International AAAI Conference on Weblogs and Social Media (ICWSM)*, Dublin, Ireland.

Marco Fisichella, Avar Stewart, Alfredo Cuzzocrea, and Kerstin Denecke. 2011. Detecting Health Events on the Social Web to Enable Epidemic Intelligence. In *Proceedings of the International Symposium on String Processing and Information Retrieval (SPIRE)*, pages 87–103, Pisa, Italy.

Birgit Hamp and Helmut Feldweg. 1997. GermaNet - a Lexical-Semantic Net for German. In *Proceedings of ACL workshop Automatic Information Extraction and Building of Lexical Semantic Resources for NLP Applications*, pages 9–15, Madrid, Spain.

Vasileios Hatzivassiloglou and Kathleen R. McKeown. 1997. Predicting the Semantic Orientation of Adjectives. In *Proceedings of the Conference on European Chapter of the Association for Computational Linguistics (EACL)*, pages 174–181, Madrid, Spain.

Vasileios Hatzivassiloglou and Janyce Wiebe. 2000. Effects of Adjective Orientation and Gradability on Sentence Subjectivity. In *Proceedings of the International Conference on Computational Linguistics (COLING)*, pages 299–305, Saarbrücken, Germany.

Thorsten Joachims. 1999. Making Large-Scale SVM Learning Practical. In B. Schölkopf, C. Burges, and A. Smola, editors, *Advances in Kernel Methods - Support Vector Learning*. MIT Press.

Manfred Klenner, Stefanos Petrakis, and Angela Fahrni. 2009. Robust Compositional Polarity Classification. In *Proceedings of Recent Advances in Natural Language Processing (RANLP)*, pages 180–184, Borovets, Bulgaria.

George Lakoff. 1973. Hedging: A Study in Media Criteria and the Logic of Fuzzy Concepts. *Journal of Philosophical Logic*, 2:458 – 508.

J. Richard Landis and Gary G. Koch. 1977. The Measurement of Observer Agreement for Categorical Data. *Biometrics*, 33(1):159–174.

Mitchell P. Marcus, Beatrice Santorini, and Mary Ann Marcinkiewicz. 1993. Building a Large Annotated Corpus of English: The Penn Treebank. *Computational Linguistics*, 19(2):313–330, June. Special Issue on Using Large Corpora.

Qingliang Miao, Shu Zhang, Bo Zhang, Yao Meng, and Hao Yu. 2012. Extracting and Visualizing Semantic Relationships from Chinese Biomedical Text. In *Proceedings of the Pacific Asia Conference on Language, Information and Compuation (PACLIC)*, pages 99–107, Bali, Indonesia.

George Miller, Richard Beckwith, Christiane Fellbaum, Derek Gross, and Katherine Miller. 1990. Introduction to WordNet: An On-line Lexical Database. *International Journal of Lexicography*, 3:235–244.

Roser Morante and Walter Daelemans. 2009. Learning the Scope of Hedge Cues in Biomedical Texts. In *Proceedings of the BioNLP Workshop*, pages 28–36, Boulder, CO, USA.

Robert Munro, Lucky Gunasekara, Stephanie Nevins, Lalith Polepeddi, and Evan Rosen. 2012. Tracking Epidemics with Natural Language Processing and Crowdsourcing. In *Proceedings of the Spring Symposium for Association for the Advancement of Artificial Intelligence (AAAI)*, pages 52–58, Toronto, Canada.

Anna Rafferty and Christopher D. Manning. 2008. Parsing Three German Treebanks: Lexicalized and Unlexicalized Baselines. In *Proceedings of the ACL Workshop on Parsing German (PaGe)*, pages 40–46, Columbus, OH, USA.

Anne Schiller, Simone Teufel, Christine Stöckert, and Christine Thielen. 1995. Vorläufige Guidelines für das Tagging deutscher Textcorpora mit STTS. Technical report, Universität Stuttgart, Insitut für maschinelle Sprachverarbeitung, and Seminar für Sprachwissenschaft, Universität Tübingen.

Maite Taboada, Julian Brooke, Milan Tofiloski, Kimberly Voll, and Manfred Stede. 2011. Lexicon-Based Methods for Sentiment Analysis. *Computational Linguistics*, 37(2):267 – 307.

Manabu Torii, Lanlan Yin, Thang Nguyen, Chand T. Mazumdar, Hongfang Liu, David M. Hartley, and Noele P. Nelson. 2011. An exploratory study of a text classification framework for internet-based surveillance of emerging epidemics. *Internal Journal of Medical Informatics*, 80(1):56–66.

Willem Robert van Hage, Sophia Katrenko, and Guus Schreiber. 2005. A Method to Combine Linguistic Ontology-Mapping Techniques. In *Proceedings of International Semantic Web Conference (ISWC)*, pages 732 – 744, Galway, Ireland. Springer.

Willem Robert van Hage, Hap Kolb, and Guus Schreiber. 2006. A Method for Learning Part-Whole Relations. In *Proceedings of International Semantic Web Conference (ISWC)*, pages 723 – 735, Athens, GA, USA. Springer.

Willem Robert van Hage, Margherita Sini, Lori Finch, Hap Kolb, and Guus Schreiber. 2010. The OAEI food task: an analysis of a thesaurus alignment task. *Applied Ontology*, 5(1):1 – 28.

Janyce Wiebe and Rada Mihalcea. 2006. Word Sense and Subjectivity. In *Proceedings of the International Conference on Computational Linguistics and Annual Meeting of the Association for Computational Linguistics (COLING/ACL)*, pages 1065–1072, Syndney, Australia.

Michael Wiegand, Benjamin Roth, and Dietrich Klakow. 2012a. Web-based Relation Extraction for the Food Domain. In *Proceeding of the International Conference on Applications of Natural Language Processing to Information Systems (NLDB)*, pages 222–227, Groningen, the Netherlands. Springer.

Michael Wiegand, Benjamin Roth, Eva Lasarcyk, Stephanie Köser, and Dietrich Klakow. 2012b. A Gold Standard for Relation Extraction in the Food Domain. In *Proceedings of the Conference on Language Resources and Evaluation (LREC)*, pages 507–514, Istanbul, Turkey.

Michael Wiegand, Manfred Klenner, and Dietrich Klakow. 2013. Bootstrapping polarity classifiers with rule-based classification. *Language Resources and Evaluation*, Online First:1–40.

Theresa Wilson, Janyce Wiebe, and Paul Hoffmann. 2005. Recognizing Contextual Polarity in Phrase-level Sentiment Analysis. In *Proceedings of the Conference on Human Language Technology and Empirical Methods in Natural Language Processing (HLT/EMNLP)*, pages 347–354, Vancouver, BC, Canada.

Ian Witten and Eibe Frank. 2005. *Data Mining: Practical Machine Learning Tools and Techniques*. Morgan Kaufmann Publishers, San Francisco, US.

Yiming Yang and Jan Pederson. 1997. A Comparative Study on Feature Selection in Text Categorization. In *Proceedings the International Conference on Machine Learning (ICML)*, pages 412–420, Nashville, US.

Hui Yang, Rajesh Swaminathan, Abhishek Sharma, Vilas Ketkar, and Jason D'Silva, 2011. *Learning Structure and Schemas from Documents*, volume 375 of *Studies in Computational Intelligence*, chapter Mining Biomedical Text Towards Building a Quantitative Food-disease-gene Network, pages 205–225. Springer Berlin Heidelberg.

# Translating Government Agencies' Tweet Feeds: Specificities, Problems and (a few) Solutions

**Fabrizio Gotti, Philippe Langlais**
{gottif,felipe}@iro.umontreal.ca
RALI-DIRO
Université de Montréal
C.P. 6128, Succ Centre-Ville
Montréal (Québec) Canada
H3C 3J7

**Atefeh Farzindar**
farzindar@nlptechnologies.ca
NLP Technologies Inc.
52 Le Royer
Montréal
(Québec) Canada
H2Y 1W7

## Abstract

While the automatic translation of tweets has already been investigated in different scenarios, we are not aware of any attempt to translate tweets created by government agencies. In this study, we report the experimental results we obtained when translating 12 Twitter feeds published by agencies and organizations of the government of Canada, using a state-of-the art Statistical Machine Translation (SMT) engine as a black box translation device. We mine parallel web pages linked from the URLs contained in English-French pairs of tweets in order to create tuning and training material. For a Twitter feed that would have been otherwise difficult to translate, we report significant gains in translation quality using this strategy. Furthermore, we give a detailed account of the problems we still face, such as hashtag translation as well as the generation of tweets of legal length.

## 1 Introduction

Twitter is currently one of the most popular online social networking service after Facebook, and is the fastest-growing, with the half-a-billion user mark reached in June 2012.[1] According to Twitter's blog, no less than 65 millions of tweets are published each day, mostly in a single language (40% in English). This hinders the spread of information, a situation witnessed for instance during the Arab Spring.

Solutions for disseminating tweets in different languages have been designed. One solution consists in manually translating tweets, which of course is only viable for a very specific subset of the material appearing on Twitter. For instance, the non-profit organization *Meedan*[2] has been founded in order to organize volunteers willing to translate tweets written in Arabic on Middle East issues. Another solution consists in using machine translation. Several portals are facilitating this,[3] mainly by using Google's machine translation API.

Curiously enough, few studies have focused on the automatic translation of text produced within social networks, even though a growing number of these studies concentrate on the automated processing of messages exchanged on social networks. See (Gimpel et al., 2011) for a recent review of some of them.

Some effort has been invested in translating short text messages (SMSs). Notably, Munro (2010) describes the service deployed by a consortium of volunteer organizations named "Mission 4636" during the earthquake that struck Haiti in January 2010. This service routed SMSs alerts reporting trapped people and other emergencies to a set of volunteers who translated Haitian Creole SMSs into English, so that primary emergency responders could understand them. In Lewis (2010), the authors describe how the Microsoft translation team developed a statistical translation engine (Haitian Creole into English) in as little as 5 days, during the same tragedy.

[1] http://semiocast.com/publications/2012_07_30_Twitter_reaches_half_a_billion_accounts_140m_in_the_US

[2] http://news.meedan.net/

[3] http://www.aboutonlinetips.com/twitter-translation-tools/

Jehl (2010) addresses the task of translating English tweets into German. She concludes that the proper treatment of unknown words is of the utmost importance and highlights the problem of producing translations of up to 140 characters, the upper limit on tweet lengths. In (Jehl et al., 2012), the authors describe their efforts to collect bilingual tweets from a stream of tweets acquired programmatically, and show the impact of such a collection on developing an Arabic-to-English translation system.

The present study participates in the effort for the dissemination of messages exchanged over Twitter in different languages, but with a very narrow focus, which we believe has not been addressed specifically yet: Translating tweets written by government institutions. What sets these messages apart is that, generally speaking, they are written in a proper language (without which their credibility would presumably be hurt), while still having to be extremely brief to abide by the ever-present limit of 140 characters. This contrasts with typical social media texts in which a large variability in quality is observed (Agichtein et al., 2008).

Tweets from government institutions can also differ somewhat from some other, more informal social media texts in their intended audience and objectives. Specifically, such tweet feeds often attempt to serve as a credible source of timely information presented in a way that engages members of the lay public. As such, translations should present a similar degree of credibility, ease of understanding, and ability to engage the audience as in the source tweet—all while conforming to the 140 character limits.

This study attempts to take these matters into account for the task of translating Twitter feeds emitted by Canadian governmental institutions. This could prove very useful, since more than 150 Canadian agencies have official feeds. Moreover, while only counting 34 million inhabitants, Canada ranks fifth in the number of Twitter users (3% of all users) after the US, the UK, Australia, and Brazil.[4] This certainly explains why Canadian governments, politicians and institutions are making an increasing use of this social network service. Given the need of Canadian governmental institutions to disseminate information in both official languages (French and English), we see a great potential value in targeted computer-aided translation tools, which could offer a significant reduction over the current time and effort required to manually translate tweets.

We show that a state-of-the-art SMT toolkit, used off-the-shelf, and trained on out-domain data is unsurprisingly not up to the task. We report in Section 2 our efforts in mining bilingual material from the Internet, which proves eventually useful in significantly improving the performance of the engine. We test the impact of simple adaptation scenarios in Section 3 and show the significant improvements in BLEU scores obtained thanks to the corpora we mined. In Section 4, we provide a detailed account of the problems that remain to be solved, including the translation of hashtags (#-words) omnipresent in tweets and the generation of translations of legal lengths. We conclude this work-in-progress and discuss further research avenues in Section 5.

## 2 Corpora

### 2.1 Bilingual Twitter Feeds

An exhaustive list of Twitter feeds published by Canadian government agencies and organizations can be found on the GOV.PoliTWiTTER.ca web site.[5] As of this writing, 152 tweet feeds are listed, most of which are available in both French and English, in keeping with the Official Languages Act of Canada. We manually selected 20 of these feed pairs, using various exploratory criteria, such as their respective government agency, the topics being addressed and, importantly, the perceived degree of parallelism between the corresponding French and English feeds.

All the tweets of these 20 feed pairs were gathered using Twitter's Streaming API on 26 March 2013. We filtered out the tweets that were marked by the API as retweets and replies, because they rarely have an official translation. Each pair of filtered feeds was then aligned at the tweet level in order to create bilingual tweet pairs. This step was facilitated by the fact that timestamps are assigned to each tweet. Since a tweet and its translation are typi-

[4] http://www.techvibes.com/blog/how-canada-stacks-up-against-the-world-on-twitter-2012-10-17

[5] http://gov.politwitter.ca/directory/network/twitter

| Tweets | URLs | *mis.* | *probs* | *sents* |
|---|---|---|---|---|
| ▷ *HealthCanada* | | | | |
| 1489 | 995 | 1 | 252 | 78,847 |
| ▷ *DFAIT_MAECI* – *Foreign Affairs and Int'l Trade* | | | | |
| 1433 | 65 | 0 | 1081 | 10,428 |
| ▷ *canadabusiness* | | | | |
| 1265 | 623 | 1 | 363 | 138,887 |
| ▷ *pmharper* – *Prime Minister Harper* | | | | |
| 752 | 114 | 2 | 364 | 12,883 |
| ▷ *TCS_SDC* – *Canadian Trade Commissioner Service* | | | | |
| 694 | 358 | 1 | 127 | 36,785 |
| ▷ *Canada_Trade* | | | | |
| 601 | 238 | 1 | 92 | 22,594 |
| ▷ *PHAC_GC* – *Public Health Canada* | | | | |
| 555 | 140 | 0 | 216 | 14,617 |
| ▷ *cida_ca* – *Canadian Int'l Development Agency* | | | | |
| 546 | 209 | 2 | 121 | 18,343 |
| ▷ *LibraryArchives* | | | | |
| 490 | 92 | 1 | 171 | 6,946 |
| ▷ *CanBorder* – *Canadian Border matters* | | | | |
| 333 | 88 | 0 | 40 | 9,329 |
| ▷ *Get_Prepared* – *Emergency preparedness* | | | | |
| 314 | 62 | 0 | 11 | 10,092 |
| ▷ *Safety_Canada* | | | | |
| 286 | 60 | 1 | 17 | 3,182 |

Table 1: Main characteristics of the Twitter and URL corpora for the 12 feed pairs we considered. The (English) feed name is underlined, and stands for the pair of feeds that are a translation of one another. When not obvious, a short description is provided. Each feed name can be found as is on Twitter. See Sections 2.1 and 2.3 for more.

cally issued at about the same time, we were able to align the tweets using a dynamic programming algorithm miminizing the total time drift between the English and the French feeds. Finally, we tokenized the tweets using an adapted version of `Twokenize` (O'Connor et al., 2010), accounting for the hashtags, usernames and urls contained in tweets.

We eventually had to narrow down further the number of feed pairs of interest to the 12 most prolific ones. For instance, the feed pair *PassportCan*[6] that we initially considered contained only 54 pairs of English-French tweets after filtering and alignment, and was discarded because too scarce.

[6]`https://twitter.com/PassportCan`

| |
|---|
| Did you know it's best to test for #radon in the fall/winter? `http://t.co/CDubjbpS` #health #safety |
| L'automne/l'hiver est le meilleur moment pour tester le taux de radon. `http://t.co/4NJWJmuN` #santé #sécurite |

Figure 1: Example of a pair of tweets extracted from the feed pair *HealthCanada*.

The main characteristics of the 12 feed pairs we ultimately retained are reported in Table 1, for a total of 8758 tweet pairs. The largest feed, in terms of the number of tweet pairs used, is that of Health Canada[7] with over 1 489 pairs of retained tweets pairs at the time of acquisition. For reference, that is 62% of the 2 395 "raw" tweets available on the English feed, before filtering and alignment. An example of a retained pair of tweets is shown in Figure 1. In this example, both tweets contain a shortened url alias that (when expanded) leads to webpages that are parallel. Both tweets also contain so-called hashtags (#-words): 2 of those are correctly translated when going from English to French, but the hashtag *#radon* is not translated into a hashtag in French, instead appearing as the plain word *radon*, for unknown reasons.

## 2.2 Out-of-domain Corpora: Parliament Debates

We made use of two different large corpora in order to train our baseline SMT engines. We used the 2M sentence pairs of the Europarl version 7 corpus.[8] This is a priori an out-of-domain corpus, and we did not expect much of the SMT system trained on this dataset. Still, it is one of the most popular parallel corpus available to the community and serves as a reference.

We also made use of 2M pairs of sentences we extracted from an in-house version of the Canadian Hansard corpus. This material is not completely out-of-domain, since the matters addressed within the Canadian Parliament debates likely coincide to some degree with those tweeted by Canadian institutions. The main characteristics of these two corpora are reported in Table 2. It is noteworthy that while both

[7]`https://twitter.com/HealthCanada`

[8]`http://www.statmt.org/europarl/`

| Corpus | | sents | tokens | types | $s$ length |
|---|---|---|---|---|---|
| hansard | en | 2M | 27.1M | 62.2K | 13.6 |
| hansard | fr | 2M | 30.7M | 82.2K | 15.4 |
| europarl | en | 2M | 55.9M | 94.5K | 28.0 |
| europarl | fr | 2M | 61.6M | 129.6K | 30.8 |

Table 2: Number of sentence pairs, token and token types in the out-of-domain training corpora we used. $s$ length stands for the average sentence length, counted in tokens.

corpora contain an equal number of sentence pairs, the average sentence length in the Europarl corpus is much higher, leading to a much larger set of tokens.

### 2.3 In-domain Corpus: URL Corpus

As illustrated in Figure 1, many tweets act as "teasers", and link to web pages containing (much) more information on the topic the tweet feed typically addresses. Therefore, a natural way of adapting a corpus-driven translation engine consists in mining the parallel text available at those urls.

In our case, we set aside the last 200 tweet pairs of each feed as a test corpus. The rest serves as the url-mining corpus. This is necessary to avoid testing our system on test tweets whose URLs have contributed to the training corpus.

Although simple in principle, this data collection operation consists in numerous steps, outlined below:

1. Split each feed pair in two: The last 200 tweet pairs are set aside for testing purposes, the rest serves as the url-mining corpus used in the following steps.

2. Isolate urls in a given tweet pair using our tokenizer, adapted to handle Twitter text (including urls).

3. Expand shortened urls. For instance, the url in the English example of Figure 1 would be expanded into `http://www.hc-sc.gc.ca/ewh-semt/radiation/radon/testing-analyse-eng.php`, using the expansion service located at the domain `t.co`. There are 330 such services on the Web.

4. Download the linked documents.

5. Extract all text from the web pages, without targeting any content in particular (the site menus, breadcrumb, and other elements are therefore retained).

6. Segment the text into sentences, and tokenize them into words.

7. Align sentences with our in-house aligner.

We implemented a number of restrictions during this process. We did not try to match urls in cases where the number of urls in each tweet differed (see column *mis.*—mismatches—in Table 1). The column *probs.* (problems) in Table 1 shows the count of url pairs whose content could not be extracted. This happened when we encountered urls that we could not expand, as well as those returning a 404 HTTP error code. We also rejected urls that were identical in both tweets, because they obviously could not be translations. We also filtered out documents that were not in html format, and we removed document pairs where at least one document was difficult to convert into text (e.g. because of empty content, or problematic character encoding). After inspection, we also decided to discard sentences that counted less than 10 words, because shorter sentences are too often irrelevant website elements (menu items, breadcrumbs, copyright notices, etc.).

This 4-hour long operation (including download) yielded a number of useful web documents and extracted sentence pairs reported in Table 1 (columns URLs and *sents* respectively). We observed that the density of url pairs present in pairs of tweets varies among feeds. Still, for all feeds, we were able to gather a set of (presumably) parallel sentence pairs.

The validity of our extraction process rests on the hypothesis that the documents mentioned in each pair of urls are parallel. In order to verify this, we manually evaluated (a posteriori) the parallelness of a random sample of 50 sentence pairs extracted for each feed. Quite fortunately, the extracted material was of excellent quality, with most samples containing all perfectly aligned sentences. Only *canadabusiness*, *LibraryArchives* and *CanBorder* counted a single mistranslated pair. Clearly, the websites of the Canadian institutions we mined are translated with great care and the tweets referring to them are meticulously translated in terms of content links.

## 3 Experiments

### 3.1 Methodology

All our translation experiments were conducted with Moses' EMS toolkit (Koehn et al., 2007), which in turn uses gizapp (Och and Ney, 2003) and SRILM (Stolcke, 2002).

As a test bed, we used the 200 bilingual tweets we acquired that were not used to follow urls, as described in Sections 2.1 and 2.3. We kept each feed separate in order to measure the performance of our system on each of them. Therefore we have 12 test sets.

We tested two configurations: one in which an out-of-domain translation system is applied (without adaptation) to the translation of the tweets of our test material, another one where we allowed the system to look at in-domain data, either at training or at tuning time. The in-domain material we used for adapting our systems is the URL corpus we described in section 2.3. More precisely, we prepared 12 tuning corpora, one for each feed, each containing 800 heldout sentence pairs. The same number of sentence pairs was considered for out-domain tuning sets, in order not to bias the results in favor of larger sets. For adaptation experiments conducted at training time, all the URL material extracted from a specific feed (except for the sentences of the tuning sets) was used. The language model used in our experiments was a 5-gram language model with Kneser-Ney smoothing.

It must be emphasized that there is no tweet material in our training or tuning sets. One reason for this is that we did not have enough tweets to populate our training corpus. Also, this corresponds to a realistic scenario where we want to translate a Twitter feed without first collecting tweets from this feed.

We use the BLEU metric (Papineni et al., 2002) as well as word-error rate (WER) to measure translation quality. A good translation system maximizes BLEU and minimizes WER. Due to initially poor results, we had to refine the tokenizer mentioned in Section 2.1 in order to replace urls with serialized placeholders, since those numerous entities typically require rule-based translations. The BLEU and WER scores we report henceforth were computed on such lowercased, tokenized and serialized texts, and did not incur penalties that would have otherwise been caused by the non-translation of urls (unknown tokens), for instance.

| train | tune | *canadabusiness* | | *DFAIT_MAECI* | |
|---|---|---|---|---|---|
| fr→en | | wer | bleu | wer | bleu |
| hans | hans | 59.58 | 21.16 | 61.79 | 19.55 |
| hans | in | 58.70 | 21.35 | 60.73 | 20.14 |
| euro | euro | 64.24 | 15.88 | 62.90 | 17.80 |
| euro | in | 63.23 | 17.48 | 60.58 | 21.23 |
| en→fr | | wer | bleu | wer | bleu |
| hans | hans | 62.42 | 21.71 | 64.61 | 21.43 |
| hans | in | 61.97 | 22.92 | 62.69 | 22.00 |
| euro | euro | 64.66 | 19.52 | 63.91 | 21.65 |
| euro | in | 64.61 | 18.84 | 63.56 | 22.31 |

Table 3: Performance of generic systems versus systems adapted at tuning time for two particular feeds. The tune corpus "in" stands for the URL corpus specific to the feed being translated. The tune corpora "hans" and "euro" are considered out-of-domain for the purpose of this experiment.

### 3.2 Translation Results

Table 3 reports the results observed for the two main configurations we tested, in both translation directions. We show results only for two feeds here: *canadabusiness*, for which we collected the largest number of sentence pairs in the URL corpus, and *DFAIT_MAECI* for which we collected very little material. For *canadabusiness*, the performance of the system trained on Hansard data is higher than that of the system trained on Europarl ($\Delta$ ranging from 2.19 to 5.28 points of BLEU depending on the configuration considered). For *DFAIT_MAECI*, suprisingly, Europarl gives a better result, but by a more narrow margin ($\Delta$ ranging from 0.19 to 1.75 points of BLEU). Both tweet feeds are translated with comparable performance by SMT, both in terms of BLEU and WER. When comparing BLEU performances based solely on the tuning corpus used, the in-domain tuning corpus created by mining urls yields better results than the out-domain tuning corpus seven times out of eight for the results shown in Table 3.

The complete results are shown in Figure 2, showing BLEU scores obtained for the 12 feeds we considered, when translating from English to French. Here, the impact of using in-domain data to tune

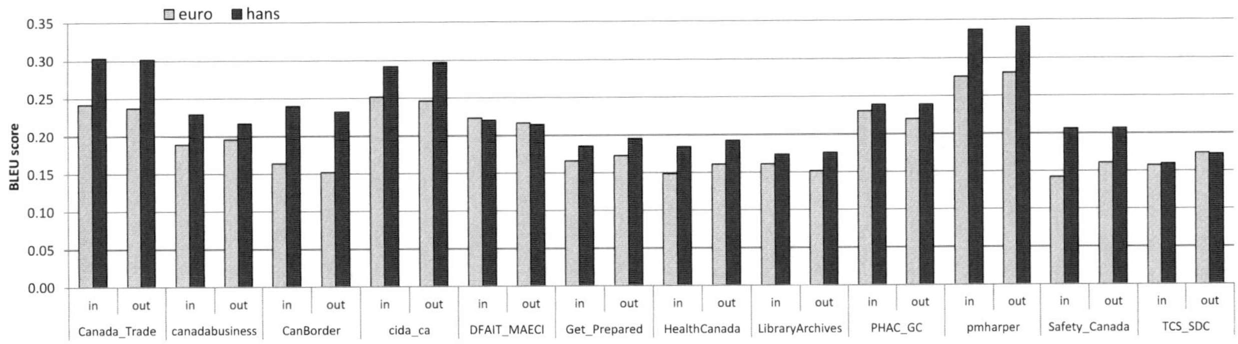


Figure 2: BLEU scores measured on the 12 feed pairs we considered for the English-to-French translation direction. For each tweet test corpus, there are 4 results: a dark histogram bar refers to the Hansard training corpus, while a lighter grey bar refers to an experiment where the training corpus was Europarl. The "in" category on the $x$-axis designates an experiment where the tuning corpus was in-domain (URL corpus), while the "out" category refers to an out-of-domain tuning set. The out-of-domain tuning corpus is Europarl or Hansard, and always matches the nature of training corpora.

the system is hardly discernible, which in a sense is good news, since tuning a system for each feed is not practical. The Hansard corpus almost always gives better results, in keeping with its status as a corpus that is not so out-of-domain as Europarl, as mentioned above. The results for the reverse translation direction show the same trends.

In order to try a different strategy than using only tuning corpora to adapt the system, we also investigated the impact of training the system on a mix of out-of-domain and in-domain data. We ran one of the simplest adaptation scenarios where we concatenated the in-domain material (train part of the URL corpus) to the out-domain one (Hansard corpus) for the two feeds we considered in Table 3. The results are reported in Table 4.

We measured significant gains both in WER and BLEU scores in conducting training time versus tuning time adaptation, for the *canadabusiness* feed (the largest URL corpus). For this corpus, we observe an interesting gain of more than 6 absolute points in BLEU scores. However, for the *DFAIT_MAECI* (the smallest URL corpus) we note a very modest loss in translation quality when translating from French and a significant gain in the other translation direction. These figures could show that mining parallel sentences present in URLs is a fruitful strategy for adapting the translation engine for feeds like *canadabusiness* that display poor performance otherwise, without harming the translation quality for feeds that perform reasonably well without additional resources. Unfortunately, it suggests that retraining a system is required for better performance, which might hinder the deployment of a standalone translation engine. Further research needs to be carried out to determine how many tweet pairs must be used in a parallel URL corpus in order to get a sufficiently good in-domain corpus.

| Train corpus | WER | BLEU |
|---|---|---|
| | fr→en | |
| hans+*canbusiness* | 53.46 *(-5.24)* | 27.60 *(+6.25)* |
| hans+*DFAIT* | 60.81 *(+0.23)* | 20.83 *(-0.40)* |
| | en→fr | |
| hans+*canbusiness* | 57.07 *(-4.90)* | 26.26 *(+3.34)* |
| hans+*DFAIT* | 61.80 *(-0.89)* | 24.93 *(+2.62)* |

Table 4: Performance of systems trained on a concatenation of out-of-domain and in-domain data. All systems were tuned on in-domain data. Absolute gains are shown in parentheses, over the best performance achieved so far (see Table 3).

## 4 Analysis

### 4.1 Translation output

Examples of translations produced by the best system we trained are reported in Figure 3. The first translation shows a case of an unknown French word (*soumissionnez*). The second example illustrates a typical example where the hashtags should have been translated but were left unchanged. The third example shows a correct translation, except that the length of the translation (once the text is detokenized) is over the size limit allowed for a tweet. Those problems are further analyzed in the remaining subsections.

### 4.2 Unknown words

Unknown words negatively impact the quality of MT output in several ways. First, they typically appear untranslated in the system's output (we deemed most appropriate this last resort strategy). Secondly, they perturb the language model, which often causes other problems (such as dubious word ordering). Table 5 reports the main characteristics of the words from all the tweets we collected that were not present in the Hansard train corpus.

The out-of-vocabulary rate with respect to token types hovers around 33% for both languages. No less than 42% (resp. 37%) of the unknown English (resp. French) token types are actually hashtags. We defer their analysis to the next section. Also, 15% (resp. 10%) of unknown English token types are user names (@user), which do not require translation.

| | English | French |
|---|---|---|
| tweet tokens | 153 234 | 173 921 |
| tweet types | 13 921 | 15 714 |
| | | |
| OOV types | 4 875 *(35.0%)* | 5 116 *(32.6%)* |
| ▷ hashtag types | 2 049 *(42.0%)* | 1 909 *(37.3%)* |
| ▷ @user types | 756 *(15.5%)* | 521 *(10.2%)* |

Table 5: Statistics on out-of-vocabulary token types.

We manually analyzed 100 unknown token types that were not hashtags or usernames and that did not contain any digit. We classified them into a number of broad classes whose distributions are reported in Table 6 for the French unknown types. A similar distribution was observed for English unknown types. While we could not decide of the nature of 21 types without their context of use (line *?type*), we frequently observed English types, as well as acronyms and proper names. A few unknown types result from typos, while many are indeed true French types unseen at training time (row labeled *french*), some of which being very specific (*term*). Amusingly, the French verbal neologism *twitter* (*to tweet*) is unknown to the Hansard corpus we used.

| | | |
|---|---|---|
| french | 26 | *sautez, perforateurs, twitter* |
| english | 22 | *successful, beauty* |
| ?types | 21 | *bumbo, tra* |
| name | 11 | *absorbica, konzonguizi* |
| acronym | 7 | *hna, rnc* |
| typo | 6 | *gazouilli, pendan* |
| term | 3 | *apostasie, sibutramine* |
| foreign | 2 | *aanischaaukamikw, aliskiren* |
| others | 2 | *francophones*URL |

Table 6: Distribution of 100 unknown French token types (excluding hashtags and usernames).

### 4.3 Dealing with Hashtags

We have already seen that translating the text in hashtags is often suitable, but not always. Typically, hashtags in the middle of a sentence are to be translated, while those at the end typically should not be. A model should be designed for learning when to translate an hashtag or not. Also, some hashtags are part of the sentence, while others are just (semantic) tags. While a simple strategy for translating hashtags consists in removing the # sign at translation time, then restoring it afterwards, this strategy would fail in a number of cases that require segmenting the text of the hashtag first. Table 7 reports the percentage of hashtags that should be segmented before being translated, according to a manual analysis we conducted over 1000 hashtags in both languages we considered. While many hashtags are single words, roughly 20% of them are not and require segmentation.

### 4.4 Translating under size constraints

The 140 character limit Twitter imposes on tweets is well known and demands a certain degree of concision even human users find sometimes bothersome. For machine output, this limit becomes a challenging problem. While there exists plain–but inelegant–workarounds[9], there may be a way to *produce* tweet translations that are themselves Twitter-ready. (Jehl,

[9]The service eztweets.com splits long tweets into smaller ones; twitlonger.com tweets the beginning of a long message,

SRC: vous soumissionnez pour obtenir de gros contrats ? voici 5 pratiques exemplaires à suivre . URL
TRA: you soumissionnez big contracts for best practices ? here is 5 URL to follow .
REF: bidding on big contracts ? here are 5 best practices to follow . URL

SRC: avis de #santépublique : maladies associées aux #salmonelles et à la nourriture pour animaux de compagnie URL #rappel
TRA: notice of #santépublique : disease associated with the #salmonelles and pet food #rappel URL
REF: #publichealth notice : illnesses related to #salmonella and #petfood URL #recall

SRC: des haïtiens de tous les âges , milieux et métiers témoignent de l' aide qu' ils ont reçue depuis le séisme . URL #haïti
TRA: the haitian people of all ages and backgrounds and trades testify to the assistance that they have received from the earthquake #haïti URL .
REF: #canada in #haiti : haitians of all ages , backgrounds , and occupations tell of the help they received . URL

Figure 3: Examples of translations produced by an engine trained on a mix of in- and out-of-domain data.

| w. | en | fr | example |
|---|---|---|---|
| 1 | 76.5 | 79.9 | *intelligence* |
| 2 | 18.3 | 11.9 | *gender equality* |
| 3 | 4.0 | 6.0 | *africa trade mission* |
| 4 | 1.0 | 1.4 | *closer than you think* |
| 5 | 0.2 | 0.6 | *i am making a difference* |
| 6 | – | 0.2 | *fonds aide victime sécheresse afrique est* |

Table 7: Percentage of hashtags that require segmentation prior to translation. *w.* stands for the number of words into which the hashtag text should be segmented.

2010) pointed out this problem and reported that 3.4% of tweets produced were overlong, when translating from German to English. The reverse directions produced 17.2% of overlong German tweets. To remedy this, she tried modifying the way BLEU is computed to penalize long translation during the tuning process, with BLEU scores worse than simply truncating the illegal tweets. The second strategy the author tried consisted in generating $n$-best lists and mining them to find legal tweets, with encouraging results (for $n = 30\,000$), since the number of overlong tweets was significantly reduced while leaving BLEU scores unharmed.

In order to assess the importance of the problem for our system, we measured the lengths of tweets that a system trained like hans+*canbusiness* in Table 4 (a mix of in- and out-of-domain data) could produce. This time however, we used a larger test set counting 498 tweets. To measure the lengths of their translations, we first had to detokenize the translations produced, since the limitation applies to "natural" text only. For each URL serialized token, we counted 18 characters, the average length of a (shortened) url in a tweet. When translating from French to English, the 498 translations had lengths ranging from 45 to 138 characters; hence, they were all legal tweets. From English to French, however, the translations are longer, and range from 32 characters to 223 characters, with 22.5% of them overlong.

One must recall that in our experiments, no tweets were seen at training or tuning time, which explains why the rate of translations that do not meet the limit is high. This problem deserves a specific treatment for a system to be deployed. One interesting solution already described by (Jehl, 2010) is to mine the $n$-best list produced by the decoder in order to find the first candidate that constitutes a legal tweet. This candidate is then picked as the translation. We performed this analysis on the *canadabusiness* output described earlier, from English to French. We used $n$ =1, 5, 10, 20, 50, 100, 200, 500, 1000, 5000, 10000, 30000 and computed the resulting BLEU scores and remaining percentage of overlong tweets. The results are shown in Figure 4. The results clearly show that the $n$-best list does contain alternate candidates when the best one is too long. Indeed, not only do we observe that the percentage of remaining illegal tweets can fall steadily (from 22.4% to 6.6% for $n = 30\,000$) as we dig deeper into the list, but also the BLEU score stays unharmed, showing even a slight improvement, from an ini-

and provides a link to read the remainder. One could also simply truncate an illegal tweet and hope for the best...

tial 26.16 to 26.31 for $n = 30\,000$. This counter-intuitive result in terms of BLEU is also reported in (Jehl, 2010) and is probably due to a less harsh brevity penalty by BLEU on shorter candidates.

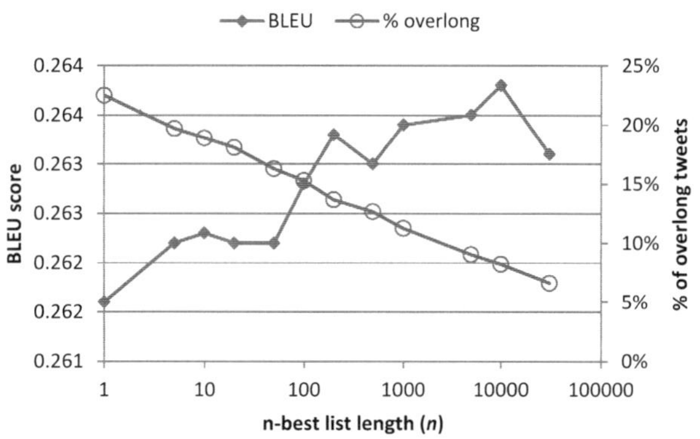


Figure 4: BLEU scores and percentage of overlong tweets when mining the $n$-best list for legal tweets, when the first candidate is overlong. The BLEU scores (diamond series) should be read off the left-hand vertical axis, while the remaining percentage of illegal tweets (circle series) should be read off the right-hand axis.

## 5 Discussion

We presented a number of experiments where we translated tweets produced by Canadian governments institutions and organizations. Those tweets have the distinguishing characteristic (in the Twitter-sphere) of being written in proper English or French. We show that mining the urls mentioned in those tweets for parallel sentences can be a fruitful strategy for adapting an out-of-domain translation engine to this task, although further research could show other ways of using this resource, whose quality seems to be high according to our manual evaluation. We also analyzed the main problems that remain to be addressed before deploying a useful system.

While we focused here on acquiring useful corpora for adapting a translation engine, we admit that the adaptation scenario we considered is very simplistic, although efficient. We are currently investigating the merit of different methods to adaptation (Zhao et al., 2004; Foster et al., 2010; Daume III and Jagarlamudi, 2011; Razmara et al., 2012; Sankaran et al., 2012).

Unknown words are of concern, and should be dealt with appropriately. The serialization of urls was natural, but it could be extended to usernames. The latter do not need to be translated, but reducing the vocabulary is always desirable when working with a statistical machine translation engine. One interesting subcategories of out-of-vocabulary tokens are hashtags. According to our analysis, they require segmentation into words before being translated in 20% of the cases. Even if they are transformed into regular words (#radon→radon or #genderequality→gender equality), however, it is not clear at this point how to detect if they are used like normally-occurring words in a sentence, as in (#radon is harmful) or if they are simply tags added to the tweet to categorize it.

We also showed that translating under size constraints can be handled easily by mining the $n$-best list produced by the decoder, but only up to a point. A remaining 6% of the tweets we analyzed in detail could not find a shorter version. Numerous ideas are possible to alleviate the problem. One could for instance modify the logic of the decoder to penalize hypotheses that promise to yield overlong translations. Another idea would be to manually inspect the strategies used by governmental agencies on Twitter when attempting to shorten their messages, and to select those that seem acceptable and implementable, like the suppression of articles or the use of authorized abbreviations.

Adapting a translation pipeline to the very specific world of governmental tweets therefore poses multiple challenges, each of which can be addressed in numerous ways. We have reported here the results of a modest but fertile subset of these adaptation strategies.

## Acknowledgments

This work was funded by a grant from the Natural Sciences and Engineering Research Council of Canada. We also wish to thank Houssem Eddine Dridi for his help with the Twitter API.

## References


Eugene Agichtein, Carlos Castillo, Debora Donato, Aristides Gionis, and Gilad Mishne. 2008. Finding high-quality content in social media. In *Proceedings of the 2008 International Conference on Web Search and Data Mining*, WSDM '08, pages 183–194.

Hal Daume III and Jagadeesh Jagarlamudi. 2011. Domain adaptation for machine translation by mining unseen words. In *49th ACL*, pages 407–412, Portland, Oregon, USA, June.

George Foster, Cyril Goutte, and Roland Kuhn. 2010. Discriminative instance weighting for domain adaptation in statistical machine translation. In *EMNLP*, pages 451–459, Cambridge, MA, October.

Kevin Gimpel, Nathan Schneider, Brendan O'Connor, Dipanjan Das, Daniel Mills, Jacob Eisenstein, Michael Heilman, Dani Yogatama, Jeffrey Flanigan, and Noah A. Smith. 2011. Part-of-speech tagging for twitter: Annotation, features, and experiments. In *ACL (Short Papers)*, pages 42–47.

Laura Jehl, Felix Hieber, and Stefan Riezler. 2012. Twitter translation using translation-based cross-lingual retrieval. In *7th Workshop on Statistical Machine Translation*, pages 410–421, Montréal, June.

Laura Jehl. 2010. Machine translation for twitter. Master's thesis, School of Philosophie, Psychology and Language Studies, University of Edinburgh.

Philipp Koehn, Hieu Hoang, Alexandra Birch, Chris Callison-burch, Richard Zens, Rwth Aachen, Alexandra Constantin, Marcello Federico, Nicola Bertoldi, Chris Dyer, Brooke Cowan, Wade Shen, Christine Moran, and Ondřej Bojar. 2007. Moses: Open source toolkit for statistical machine translation. pages 177–180.

William D. Lewis. 2010. Haitian creole: How to build and ship an mt engine from scratch in 4 days, 17 hours, & 30 minutes. In *EAMT*, Saint-Raphael.

Robert Munro. 2010. Crowdsourced translation for emergency response in Haiti: the global collaboration of local knowledge. In *AMTA Workshop on Collaborative Crowdsourcing for Translation*, Denver.

Franz Josef Och and Hermann Ney. 2003. A systematic comparison of various statistical alignment models. *Comput. Linguist.*, 29(1):19–51, March.

Brendan O'Connor, Michel Krieger, and David Ahn. 2010. TweetMotif: Exploratory Search and Topic Summarization for Twitter. In William W. Cohen, Samuel Gosling, William W. Cohen, and Samuel Gosling, editors, *ICWSM*. The AAAI Press.

Kishore Papineni, Salim Roukos, Todd Ward, and Wei J. Zhu. 2002. BLEU: a method for automatic evaluation of machine translation. In *Proceedings of 40th Annual Meeting of the Association for Computational Linguistics*, pages 311–318, Philadelphia, Pennsylvania, USA, July. Association for Computational Linguistics.

Majid Razmara, George Foster, Baskaran Sankaran, and Anoop Sarkar. 2012. Mixing multiple translation models in statistical machine translation. In *Proceedings of the 50th ACL*, Jeju, Republic of Korea, jul.

Baskaran Sankaran, Majid Razmara, Atefeh Farzindar, Wael Khreich, Fred Popowich, and Anoop Sarkar. 2012. Domain adaptation techniques for machine translation and their evaluation in a real-world setting. In *Proceedings of 25th Canadian Conference on Artificial Intelligence*, Toronto, Canada, may.

Andreas Stolcke. 2002. SRILM – an extensible language modeling toolkit. In *Proceedings of ICSLP*, volume 2, pages 901–904, Denver, USA.

Bing Zhao, Matthias Eck, and Stephan Vogel. 2004. Language model adaptation for statistical machine translation with structured query models. In *20th COLING*.

# Author Index

**Association for Computational Linguistics**
209 N. Eighth Street
Stroudsburg, Pennsylvania 18360

CURRAN ASSOCIATES INC
proceedings.com